M000211840

Crossing Literacy Bridges

Crossing Literacy Bridges

Strategies to Collaborate with Families of Struggling Readers

Jennifer Tuten, Deborah Ann Jensen, and Charlene Klassen Endrizzi

Foreword by

Kathryn Mitchell Pierce

ROWMAN & LITTLEFIELD
Lanham • Boulder • New York • London

Published by Rowman & Littlefield
An imprint of The Rowman & Littlefield Publishing Group, Inc.
4501 Forbes Boulevard, Suite 200, Lanham, Maryland 20706
www.rowman.com

Unit A, Whitacre Mews, 26-34 Stannary Street, London SE11 4AB

Copyright © 2018 by Jennifer Tuten, Deborah Ann Jensen, and Charlene Klassen
Endrizzi

All rights reserved. No part of this book may be reproduced in any form or by any
electronic or mechanical means, including information storage and retrieval systems,
without written permission from the publisher, except by a reviewer who may quote
passages in a review.

British Library Cataloguing in Publication Information Available

Library of Congress Cataloging-in-Publication Data Is Available

ISBN 978-1-4758-4184-8 (cloth: alk. paper)
ISBN 978-1-4758-4185-5 (pbk: alk. paper)
ISBN 978-1-4758-4186-2 (electronic)

♾️ᵀᴹ The paper used in this publication meets the minimum requirements of American
National Standard for Information Sciences—Permanence of Paper for Printed Library
Materials, ANSI/NISO Z39.48-1992.

Printed in the United States of America

Contents

Foreword

In *Crossing Literacy Bridges*, Jenny Tuten, Deb Jensen, and Charlene Klassen Endrizzi have written an inspiring celebration of teachers and families, and shared their decades of work supporting teachers in constructing collaborative and generative partnerships with families. The bridges metaphor invites teachers to see home–school relationships as taking place through two-way communication, connecting those who are dedicated to the literacy learning success of the child at home and at school. The authors recognize that these bridges require careful construction and regular maintenance if they are to be successful—and then they show us how this work might unfold.

Permeating the text is a strong respect for teachers, for literacy learners, and for their families. Within this respectful context, the authors challenge readers to reflect on their own assumptions about families, to critique the ways school invitations may mismatch with home cultures, and to join with others to build stronger home–school partnerships.

Joyce Epstein's (1995) foundational work has established the need for schools to reach out to families in meaningful ways and to invite them to become partners in the education of our children. Still, teachers are hungry for ideas to build these important relationships. Parent conferences are fairly common practice in many schools throughout the United States, and yet so much of the interactions between home and school reflect a one-way stream of communication from school to home. Teachers and schools send information home *to* families. They explain assessment results *to* families. They provide strategies *to* families so that they can help their children at home with school-related tasks and skills.

This one-way communication is even stronger when the focus is on children who struggle with school literacy. Teachers anxious to help students "catch up" or "close the gap" implore families to work on reading skills at home, offering a wealth of tasks and materials to support this *home* work. The authors begin with a critical reflection on the use of the term *struggling* to describe readers, and justify their use of the term in this text. While acknowledging that some readers do indeed struggle with the learning-to-read process, the authors point out that these struggles can be the result of teaching methods, teacher assumptions, or testing processes that perpetuate a deficit view of students who develop literacy at a different rate or in different ways from their peers. In addition, the authors acknowledge the cultural, linguistic, and power differences between home and school that make it challenging to build bridges, and call upon teachers to create structures that allow both groups to overcome these barriers.

Through vignettes featuring teachers and families, the authors show us what is possible when schools invite families into these essential two-way conversations about children's literacy learning. What captured my attention from the start was the deeply respectful way they celebrate innovative teachers and honor the rich, diverse home cultures of families. Building on the foundational work of Luis Moll (2005), who taught us to respect the "funds of knowledge" that families and communities have developed, the authors invite readers to witness the ways teachers can learn from and with families in their joint commitment to children.

The core chapters of the book are based on the authors' five key principles for building successful partnerships between home and school:

1. Teachers can build literacy bridges of understanding between home and school by initiating trustworthy conversations through surveys and interviews in order to broaden their understanding of children's literate lives.
2. Teachers can build bridges of understanding between home and school by a collaborative approach to traditional home–school communications and activities.
3. Teachers can build bridges of understanding between home and school by honoring and valuing families' out-of-school literacy experiences as springboards for literacy explorations.
4. Teachers can build bridges of understanding between home and school by building and expanding on curricular explorations and adapting them to families' literacy events.
5. Teachers can build bridges of understanding between home and school by recognizing and celebrating families' cultural diversity through building on the power of storytelling and family stories.

Each chapter begins with a thought-provoking vignette that introduces the key principle, followed by a useful review of the relevant professional literature and detailed descriptions of successful strategies the authors have gathered and constructed through their extensive work with schools and families. Chapter summaries and "3, 2, 1 Stop and Think" invitations make the book even more accessible to preservice and early career teachers. I particularly appreciated the textboxes that include detailed examples of teacher language to promote respectful relationships, teacher analysis of information gathered from families, charts that summarize key points, and resources for learning more. The thoughtful organization of this book makes it an ideal choice for students in graduate or undergraduate courses focused on family partnerships, or for teachers engaged in study groups or other professional development experiences.

Few would question the value of building relationships with families, particularly in our efforts to support those children who seem to be struggling with literacy learning in school. Jenny, Deb, and Charlene challenge us to critically examine the assumptions we have about families—particularly those whose cultural practices are significantly different from our own. Through the power of stories, the authors then show us how we might begin to engage families in more powerful partnerships.

Kathryn Mitchell Pierce
Saint Louis University
April 2018

Preface

Our book shares vivid stories of teachers and families building strong learning partnerships. It seems only fitting to introduce this book with the story of the beginning of our partnership.

Deborah and Jenny, literacy education professors and colleagues, presented their investigations about teachers and families in an after-school literacy program at NCTE's November 2005 conference in Pittsburgh. Charlene, who presented her inquiry with families and preservice teachers, approached them after the session with great questions, leading to good conversations (and recommendations for wonderful Pittsburgh restaurants!). Through subsequent discussions, we discovered common teaching practices and journeys of working with children and families; thus a friendship emerged.

Since 2005, we have regularly presented research interests together at conferences; the critical yet rarely addressed focus on literacy and families remains at the center of our work.

As a professor of literacy education, Charlene works with undergraduate and graduate students, teachers, and families to create family–school literacy partnerships. In a recent four-year teacher research project, she helped classroom teachers and student teachers construct learning engagements with families from diverse backgrounds. Ongoing conversations and dialogue enabled teachers and families to realize the importance of each other's unique literacy interactions with children. Family literacy gatherings focused on helping teachers explain their literacy curriculum, and family literacy photo projects, aimed at gathering evidence of home literacy practices, remain at the heart of her inquiry.

Over the past ten years, Jenny and Deborah have coordinated an after-school program, Literacy Space, where graduate students (practicing teachers pursuing a degree in literacy education) tutored struggling readers for one year. Their work has focused on the assessments and intervention strategies necessary to help the children acquire greater literacy proficiency in school. They recognized the essential role of families with the struggling readers as partners in the literacy learning process. Graduate students wrote letters to the families of their students, made games for their tutees, and then hosted games nights, literacy celebrations, and parent/family workshops. Graduate students soon realized how pivotal doorway conversations with families informed their work with struggling readers. Building on this extensive practical experience led Jenny and Deborah to develop new understandings and practices in forming family–teacher partnerships.

Over the years, we have continued to challenge each other's work, ask questions for understanding, and encourage each other. Over dinners in a variety of cities, we have shared stories of work with colearners—families, children, and teachers. We regularly explore insights from professional readings, workshops, and observations in educational settings. We also exchange stories of their children as literacy learners inside and outside of school.

While outlining the beginning of this book over dinner a year ago, we uncovered similar guiding understandings. Looking at our work collectively, we extracted commonalities and principles that inform our practice and support teachers in building strong relationships with the families. Thus five guiding principles of learning alongside families of struggling readers emerged as the central theme of this book. We wholeheartedly agree with Donald Graves's sentiment that teachers and families need each other. We hope these five principles, coupled with practical instructional strategies, nudge you forward in your work with families and readers.

Acknowledgments

Our understanding of home–school partnerships continues to evolve in our work alongside families and their children. For Jenny and Deborah, the students and families attending Literacy Space became invaluable sources of inspiration and knowledge. For Charlene, the families and students attending many family literacy gatherings generated new perspectives.

Mallory Locke, literacy coach, doctoral student, and critical friend, played a key role in the development of this book. We all owe a great thanks to her coaching expertise, sense of humor, and command of Google Drive!

Our editor, Carlie Wall, has always been there to answer our many, many questions.

JENNY TUTEN

I am extremely fortunate to teach, think, coach, write, and learn with so many exceptional educators. In particular, I recognize the dedicated New York City teachers who shared their expertise with me for this project: Katherine Norelli, Tricia Krivac, Lauren Tzadok, Maria McAndrews, Julia Dweck, Molly O'Shea, and Ciara Whelan.

Mr. Dimitres Pantelidis is an extraordinary school principal who has been generous with his time and expertise in many professional partnerships.

Finally, many thanks to Hunter College President Jennifer J. Raab, Provost Lon Kaufman, and Dean Michael Middleton for their support of this project.

DEBORAH JENSEN

The routine of reading to me before naps and at bedtime began as soon as my parents brought me home from the hospital. Despite being teased, my mom started with a collection of children's stories she had as a child and moved to all sorts of stories in the Golden Books. As a young child, I remember stories of trains and tugboats, Ferdinand, Madeleine, and Mrs. Piggle Wiggle. Thank you, Virginia M. Jensen, for ignoring the teasing, for reading to me, and for beginning my long journey into books.

CHARLENE KLASSEN ENDRIZZI

A four-year teacher research inquiry inspired the notion of building literacy bridges, allowing me to learn with and from three distinct entities. Clairton kindergarten teachers Vicki Tekac, Lisa Jackson, Nick Glatzer, and Roxanne Tarcy graciously welcomed student teachers into their teaching lives. Fifteen inquisitive Westminster College student teachers generated innovative family–school engagements to actualize our Bridges to Reading collaboration: Abby Buckholt, Ashley Cable, Megan Carlton, Arianna Carr, Jessica Cromer, Caitlin Fleckenstein, Liz Frames, Olivia Hvizdos, Liz Ishman, Lauren McClinton, Morgan McNeal, Shanay Phillian, Marina Rozick, Emily Scharf, and Jessie Szakacs. Yet the heart of our partnership evolved from continual conversations with more than sixty Clairton kindergarten families and children who risked revealing their out-of-school literacy lives, thereby deepening our understanding of the vital role of family–school literacy partnerships.

Finally, I am grateful to Westminster College for offering support through the Hoon Faculty Development Award and the Drinko Center for Undergraduate Research.

Chapter 1

Crossing Literacy Bridges

Marta Hernandez, a recent immigrant from Mexico, waited quietly outside the college classroom with her eight-year-old son, Patrick, scheduled to begin an after-school tutoring program. Her son's first grade teacher recently indicated that her son was struggling with reading. Moreover, she had used the labels "1" and "D" to indicate he was in danger of being held back in first grade. Marta found these numbers and letters bewildering.

What does it mean to be a "1"? To be a "D"? Marta made sure that Patrick got to school on time, completed his homework, and understood the importance of learning. Because English was not her primary language, she did not feel confident that she understood the teacher's reading concerns, outlined during their recent parent–teacher conference. She hoped that coming to the tutoring program would help Patrick improve his reading skills. And she also hoped she would be able to understand his reading struggles and learn some strategies for supporting him at home.

Inside the college classroom, Carla Henderson, Patrick's teacher and a graduate student, prepared to meet Patrick and his mom. A second-year fourth grade teacher, she felt nervous about working with a younger student and interacting with his mom. While she was beginning to feel more confident about her classroom management and instruction, interacting with parents was anxiety producing. Although she believed that family involvement was important, she also felt underprepared and unsure how to speak with families or plan home–school engagement activities. She hoped that through this yearlong graduate school experience she would gain more tools and learn more effective ways to connect with families.

On different sides of the classroom door, bringing different sets of experiences and expertise to the relationship, Marta and Carla had a common goal—supporting the literacy development of Patrick. Yet, as we can see in this vignette, this is not a simple task.

Creating a literacy bridge to connect home and school learning for many teachers is difficult. In numerous schools today, the bridge linking families of struggling readers, on one side, and the school, on the other side, is fraught with controversies, disagreements, and conflicting goals.

Many factors prevent teachers and families from working together for the benefit of their struggling readers. While most teachers acknowledge that parent involvement is important, they struggle to find effective strategies for collaborating with families (believing it too difficult to get parents to cooperate and participate) (Allen, 2007; Compton-Lilly, 2003; Lareau, 2000).

Additionally, teachers feel pressure to deliver a mandated curriculum in order to get students ready for standardized tests each year. Unable to alter the curriculum to meet the individual and collective student needs in their classrooms, teachers resort to scripted lessons and limited materials to get students test ready. This serves to narrow the curriculum for many teachers, adding an additional stress.

Communication with the families of struggling readers occurs within these restrictions, frustrating both the teachers, not able to meet the needs of their struggling readers, and families of children who find literacy acquisition challenging. Teachers find themselves unable to locate the right materials or the appropriate approach. They need to discover effective ways to communicate with families of struggling readers in order to help them develop an understanding of curriculum expectations.

Just as teachers encounter difficulties, families face their own unique problems. Families in today's widely diverse schools often bring different cultural expectations to school (Delgado-Gaitan & Trueba, 1991; Compton-Lilly, 2003). Families also bring their own school histories, some with conflicting emotions about personal school failure (Edwards, Paratore, & Roser, 2009; Lawrence-Lightfoot, 2003).

Families struggle to find the right approach or materials to help their struggling readers at home and are frustrated. There is a mismatch between teachers' and families' understanding of their roles, responsibilities, and expertise. Each side of the bridge has tried to rebuild with different approaches, different materials, only to find the structure eventually weakened and in need of repairs.

Additional roadblocks occur in preservice education programs, which often provide little to no attention to building parent–teacher partnerships (Epstein & Sanders, 2007; Rochkind, Ott, Immerwahr, Doble, & Johnson, 2008). Inexperienced teachers, school cultures that do not support family–school collaboration, parents with histories of school failure, conflicts of expectations teachers have of parents and parents have of teachers, and many other disasters prevent partnerships to ensure children's academic success. Teachers and families of children having challenges acquiring proficient literacy skills present special issues when trying to form partnerships.

Many teachers and families have a view of family involvement that evolves into teachers telling families what to do with their struggling readers and writers. This is like traffic flowing only one direction on a bridge. Of the many metaphors involving a bridge, such as water under the bridge, burning your bridges, bridge over troubled water, crossing the bridge when you get to it, the meaningful ones for us are bridging gaps and building bridges between families and schools. This building ensures academic success and enhances learning and school experiences and the importance of home–school partnerships.

Mutually beneficial relationships between the school and families of struggling readers need to be purposefully constructed. It is critical for teachers to take proactive steps to listen to families' concerns and develop an understanding of the linguistic, cultural, and socioeconomic assets that families bring to the educational setting. These are important dimensions to consider when initiating open communication with families of children struggling with literacy acquisition.

Parents can provide valuable insights into their children's strengths and needs, give useful information about how their children learn, and share stories about their children while engaged in literacy activities in and out of school settings. Implementing family surveys, parent interviews, classroom newsletters, and workshops and crafting opportunities for doorway conversations, family picture book nights, memoir writing, games nights (discussed in later chapters), and other purposeful activities creates a context for families and teachers to work to unravel the literacy challenges children are experiencing in order to help struggling readers succeed.

Kuepers (n.d.) reminds us, "a bridge is a construction, something that is purposefully built and which can be perceived not only as a continuation of a road but as a place serving a special purpose on the road" (p. 4). Conversation needs to be ongoing. Parental support needs to be enlisted. As teachers, we need to be clear about our expectations and explain school culture and appropriate ways to help their children struggling with literacy acquisition. A bridge is a two-way vehicle transport, connecting two opposite sides, two groups of people, enabling the passage or connection of ideas. A bridge reduces isolation and opens up opportunity. The beauty of bridges is missed when teachers only travel in one direction. We miss the vital invitation we need to extend to travel to school or travel into the community.

As Shockley, Michalove, and Allen (1995) state, developing a partnership to travel both ways across the bridge is fundamental:

We were not trying to impose our vision of literacy but to develop relationships with families where we could learn about what already existed in the families and connect that with the literacy classroom community. We were trying to learn from parents what literacy events were important in their lives and share with them the important literacy events in their children's school. We recognized that families, as well as teachers have busy lives. We needed channels for developing meaningful partnerships that were open, dependable, and non intrusive and non evaluative. (p. 94)

INSIGHTS FROM RESEARCH

Our work with struggling readers and their families has led us on many different journeys. It has extended over many years, in different educational settings, and rests on our combined efforts in looking at what we have learned from our research into best practices. The framework we present in this book is built on a foundation of theory, experience, and learning from our successes and our failures. Each chapter presents our learning as it has challenged and carried us through our professional experiences.

Why Cross the Literacy Bridge?

The importance of home–school partnerships and its relationship to student achievement cannot be underestimated (e.g., Briggs, Jalongo, & Brown, 1997; Epstein, 1995; Lazar, Broderick, Mastilli, & Slostad, 1999; Martin & Hagan-Burke, 2002). The changing classroom population of students has made it challenging for teachers to improve test scores, meet the linguistic and learning needs of all students, and reach out to families to create educational environments in which all children are given an equal opportunity to learn.

In classrooms where teachers are not given the freedom to select educational materials, methods, and sequence, it becomes more and more difficult to meet the needs of individual students. A mandated curriculum often neglects or overlooks the diversity in literacy knowledge students, especially students struggling to become readers and writers, bring with them to school.

In addition, many instructional hours have been lost to the preparation and implementation of standardized tests such as PARCC (Partnership for Assessment of Readiness for College and Careers), causing anxiety for teachers, students, and families alike. Teachers have less time to respond to individual students and make instructional decisions best suited to their classrooms. "Standardization of education through mandated testing of selected measurable practices denies the specificity of teachers' work and students' learning, and ignores context" (Comber, 2013, p. 361).

According to Campano, Ghiso, Yee, and Pantoja (2013), "Literacy research that takes a sociocultural perspective has demonstrated the sophisticated nature of family literacy practices that, due to power differences, often are not valued in school" (p. 315). While some families may have rich culturally specific literacy practices embedded into the fabric of their everyday lives, those may not be the same practices valued or expected in accounting for school success.

Clay (1980) explained how a narrow, carefully plotted literacy curriculum dismisses the variety of pathways into literacy. These highly scripted literacy programs have often been the main source of teaching practices in resource and pull-out programs used with linguistically at-risk students. According to Luke (2011), cultural, linguistic, intellectual, and educational diversity has the potential to be flattened by standardization of practices.

Families do not need saving, a disempowering perspective. They need teachers willing to listen and consider a novel approach to building partnerships (Auerbach, 1995b; Henderson, Mapp, Johnson, & Davies 2007). In essence, teachers need to consider a stance of mutualism, where both teachers and families become vital learning partners (Cadwell, 1997; Endrizzi, 2008). The goal is not to create dichotomies but rather call for critical reflection (Auerbach, 1995b).

3, 2, 1, STOP AND THINK

3. **List three** characteristics of a *struggling reader*.
2. **Reflect and name two** barriers to your relationship with struggling readers' families.
1. **Make one** connection between your classroom's culture of working with families and the school's culture.

Who Are Struggling Readers?

Most teachers and parents can describe a struggling reader. Teachers might say, "She's not reading at grade level," or "His comprehension skills are weak." A parent might say, "He misses lots of words when he reads," or "She won't do her homework." A common profile would include a student reading below grade level or a student who appears to be disengaged from reading. Numerous books (e.g., Cooper, Chard, & Kiger, 2006; McKenna & Stahl, 2015) are available that provide tools for teachers to assess students' reading as well as strategies to support their growth (Fountas & Pinnell, 2008; Johnson & Keier, 2010; Tyner, 2009).

These texts provide a range of assessments and instructional programs for teachers. Most definitions of a struggling reader cite a student who is experiencing difficulty in reading and whose reading achievement is assessed at below grade- or age-level expectations. We recognize the current terminology of those students "striving" toward literacy acquisition. However, from our collective experience, students do struggle as they strive to become as literate as their more accomplished peers.

But beyond describing what students are not doing, what does that label mean? From our perspectives as teachers and teacher educators, we believe it is important to unpack this designation so that teachers and families better understand their students and their particular reading struggles, and are better able to support them. If we take for granted our understanding of the term, we risk limiting our understanding of students and their strengths and challenges.

Alvarez, Armstrong, Elish-Piper, Matthews, and Risko (2009) critically examine the conception of struggling readers. They argue that, too frequently, the label substitutes for inadequate or brief assessments or misalignment of curriculum or instruction and a view of reading difficulties as lying solely with the individual rather than a factor of the wider school and community context. Students may arrive with less experience in the reading strategies used or valued by the teacher in the classroom.

In doing so, the label may predetermine a deficit stance, not only potentially narrowing the instruction the student may receive but also perpetuating a negative self-image for the student. As Alvarez, Armstrong, Elish-Piper, Matthews, and Risko (2009) state, "educators will continue to fail students (rather than students failing for educators) unless educators teach to students' strengths by taking advantage of children's passions, interests, and social capital (i.e. the understandings students use in everyday life and that they bring to the classroom door)" (p. 3).

Despite the contested nature of the term *struggling*, we use it here to recognize that many students do indeed experience struggles in literacy. Johnson and Keier (2010) question the label but claim it is not necessarily a bad word; students can encounter obstacles and difficulties in the development of literacy strategies and engagement. We argue *struggle* can be embraced as part of a growth mindset (Dweck, 2007; Mraz & Hertz, 2015) when not used as a defining label.

Barriers in Forming Relationships with All Families

Teachers today face a range of student needs; culturally diverse populations; extended, blended, and alternative family structures; and a host of students who are emergent bilinguals. Some teachers have reported that they are reluctant to allow families into their classrooms, anticipating the added burden of work their presence may cause.

Some prevent parents from coming into their classrooms for fear of being judged (Richards, Frank, Sableski, & Arnold, 2016). DeCastro-Ambrosetti and Cho (2005) found teachers feared being rejected by minority parents and students and that many teachers blame the home environment and lack of value toward education for minority students' low academic performance.

The vast majority of teachers do not share the cultural, racial, or socio-economic background of the children they teach or the families they serve (Berlack & Moyenda, 2001; Catapano, 2006). An incongruity may exist between the values and norms around education held by families and the school. With this difference frequently come misunderstanding and deficit views of children and their families, resulting in a power imbalance and the inability to form partnerships.

A cultural mismatch often presents problems with effective communication. In some cultures, families would never go to school without a personal invitation (LaRocque, 2013). Teachers may fail to acknowledge the multiple ways of communicating with families. These challenges for families and teachers, on top of the difficulties many feel of having a child struggling with literacy acquisition, make the forming of partnerships hard.

Once schools and teachers actively acknowledge barriers, they can work together to put communication systems and activities into place that seek to encourage family involvement. Literacy knowledge can be demonstrated in many formats not traditionally acknowledged by all teachers. The rich literacy events in many homes are often overlooked or unknown to teachers. Both families and teachers benefit from regular, positive communication.

Families bring to the school experience a past history. Some have had negative experience with school and are angry. A family's own educational level may prevent them from feeling smart enough to interact with the teacher or school. Those challenged with their own literacy may want to avoid interacting with the school to avoid possible embarrassment (LaRocque, 2013). Some feel intimidated by the power they assume the school holds over them and their children.

Many families have two, full-time, working parents unable to attend school functions during traditional hours. These issues scream for the need for collaboration. Whether or not they do a terrific job or terrible job, whether they struggle financially or not, families have a vested interest in their children's future and success (Fullan, 2001).

Special Considerations for Families of Struggling Readers

Teachers cannot assume that families know how to help their struggling readers and may not be skilled readers themselves (Baker, 2003). Many families lack the knowledge of the educational system and proper resources to effectively support their children's learning. For example, teachers commonly urge parents to read with their children but give little guidance about what that might mean or looks like in the home (Sonnenschein & Munsterman, 2002).

There are a wide variety of constraints in forming home–school partnerships, such as a school's possible narrow definition of familial engagement or a teacher's potentially negative attitude about families being involved in the school (DeCastro-Ambrosetti & Cho, 2005; Isenberg & Jalongo, 1997), and this is a special concern for families with a struggling reader. In their study of secondary preservice and in-service teachers, DeCastro-Ambrosetti and Cho (2005) found teachers held on to the belief that the home environment and lack of value on education were responsible for students' deficient academic achievement. Yet all parents are invested in the education of their children.

Parental involvement programs, according to Auerbach (1995a), represent one of two views: a deficit view that blames the family for a lack of involvement, or a wealth view that acknowledges that all families have resources that can be used to enhance children's literacy development. If teachers want to collaborate with families, they need to seek out, understand, and build bridges to literacy practices and resources in the home.

Programs must also be culturally relevant. Culturally relevant programs begin by acknowledging a child's out-of-school experiences or funds of knowledge. In order to build a bridge to understandings about literacy, teachers need to understand parents' perceptions and beliefs about literacy learning (Goldenberg, Reese, & Gallimore, 1992). Many families benefit from learning about strategies, which can be woven into their daily lives, to support their children's literacy development. And teachers also need to inquire about families' hidden literacy experiences.

There are additional challenges in forming partnerships with families of children who are linguistically and culturally diverse and at the same time are not meeting the academic expectations in their classrooms. Mueller (2014) reported a number of roadblocks to forming working relationships with parents that teachers should keep in mind. Both verbal and nonverbal cross-cultural miscommunication may present communication barriers between parents and teachers. There are cultural assumptions about the role of families and teachers that define and sometimes limit the expectations teachers have for participation.

Often, technical educational jargon, as well as definitions of educational terminology, may frighten families and impinge on their involvement. Additionally, families "may have difficulty accessing school resources to assist their children because they have little knowledge of how the school system works" (Gaitan, 2004, p. ix). Attitudes about academic intervention for their children may carry a negative connotation and need to be addressed and explained carefully. Parents may blame themselves or their children and be frustrated with the educational system when presented with interventional needs for academic proficiency.

Family attitudes and negative connotations about a disability or a special educational need may prevent family–school collaboration (Miller & Nguyen, 2014). Some parents simply say, "My child does not need help." Limited access to interpreters and translators with proficient educational background make it difficult for non-English-speaking parents to understand and participate as partners.

According to Hollingworth and colleagues (2009), parents often feel they do not have the skills needed to support their children's academic achievement at home, and some believe that they have little influence on their children's education. Yet many at-home reading programs, and the training programs that have been held with families, have been found to be effective for struggling readers (e.g., DeFauw & Burton, 2009; Paratore & Jordan, 2007).

By reaching out to families, the teacher illustrates her commitment to helping their children struggling with literacy. A teacher can convey her vision of literacy learning as a "shared responsibility" between families and teachers (Amatea, 2013; Shockley, Michalove, & Allen, 1995) by using multiple strategies to invite uncertain readers' first learning partners back into the learning circle.

Strategies for Working with Families of Struggling Readers

An effective teacher motivates children to learn, assesses and monitors their literacy development, but also communicates to families appropriate ways to engage their children in authentic literacy tasks at home (Herold, 2011). Families are often confused by their children's inability to acquire literacy skills and many intuit that their children are not bright or that they have done something wrong to cause the problem (Lipson & Wixson, 2003).

Families need to know the difficulty with which their children are struggling in language they can understand. Often putting the blame for their children's struggles on themselves, families need to be informed that many bright, intelligent children struggle with reading and writing and progress may be slow. "Their continuing understanding of the child's work, strategies, goals, and needs, and your assessment and evaluation system, are very important to your success and the child's" (Flippo, 2003, p. 233). Ongoing dialogues with families, parental assistance, encouragement, and awareness of their children's strengths as well as needs are important to success.

DeFauw and Burton (2009) found even when parents attempted to add more support at home for their struggling reader, the lack of time was frustrating for them and for their children. Some expressed a frustration "with what they perceived as a lack of honesty teachers showed concerning their children's difficulties" (p. 34). There is often a power imbalance between parents and teachers, leaving parents frustrated and affecting their ability to actively participate (Mueller, 2014).

Programs designed for families to help them understand their children's reading challenges and friendly, easy, and simple strategies that can be woven into the families' present practices should be at the forefront in thinking about bridging literacy practices. "The intent of parent education is to empower families through information and resources so they can play active roles in their child's educational planning and delivery" (Mueller, 2014, p. 8).

When working with parents of emergent bilinguals who also struggle with literacy acquisition, education needs to be explicit about culturally embedded assumptions about schooling and school participation. Alvarez (2014) suggests teachers structure assignments so that they seek to encourage students to language broker, translate, paraphrase, and code-switch in order to recognize the language differences between home and school.

Valuing children as learners and their families as their first teachers for who they are and for what they bring into the classroom must be acknowledged. Personal and cultural frameworks may be different than those in the classroom. Children from impoverished conditions have resources that differ from the resources available to children from families with higher incomes. Children draw upon those resources; both sets of resources need to be honored. Teachers need to find ways to inquire about those resources, in order to build upon those literacy funds of knowledge.

OUR FIVE PRINCIPLES FOR WORKING WITH FAMILIES

A bridge is construction purposefully built. It is a continuing path across that which divides. We have each looked for ways to construct a two-way road in our roles as mothers, teachers, and teacher educators. Through our years of work with preservice and in-service teachers and with families of children struggling to acquire literacy skills, we have carefully constructed conversations, programs, and experiences to support the development of strong, respectful, and effective relationships between teachers and families.

Through the process of our work, we have synthesized five key terms that have guided us in our work with families: trust, collaborate, respect, adapt, and celebrate, as illustrated in figure 1.1. These have led to five principles to guide teachers as they strive to enhance their partnerships with families. Although these principles, we believe, should guide work with all families, we have found them to be particularly helpful in our work across classroom and literacy tutoring programs in urban, suburban, and rural environments.

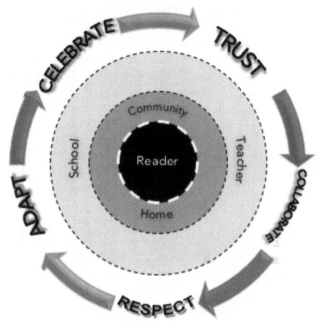

Figure 1.1. Framework of Five Principles

The concentric circles, with the reader at the center, describe the contexts and individuals critical to the reader's literacy development. The five principles encircle those relationships.

Our work with struggling readers and their families has allowed us to tailor classroom practice and communication efforts specifically to their concerns. We share examples of letters we have sent, surveys we have used, how we have organized workshops, games nights, reading recitals, all structured for families of children struggling with literacy acquisition. Each of these chapters delves into a principle in depth.

We begin by offering a story from our collective experience of working with families of struggling readers. We discuss how it lent itself to the formation of the chapter's principle. We provide a brief discussion of the research that supports the principle before delving into the insights of the practical, observable considerations we have found in our work. We end the chapter by supplying the reader with tools we have developed and used with pre-service and in-service teachers and how technology can enhance our efforts in working with families of struggling readers.

After the discussion of the principles, suggestions of children's literature as literacy bridges for families, students, and teachers and possible activities are offered. In the final chapter, we suggest activities and events to foster partnerships as well as sample materials that can be duplicated or adapted to individual classrooms. These principles, and the subsequent chapters, are springboards for your own reflection, planning, and implementation of programs for families of struggling readers at your school. We acknowledge each district, each school, and each classroom is unique. Families, teachers, community resources, and financial support for programs will be different from one location to the next. We ask that you consider how the principles we offer here can best work in your educational environment.

Our five principles are the following:

1. *Teachers can build literacy bridges of understanding between home and school by initiating trustworthy conversations through surveys and interviews in order to broaden their understanding of children's literate lives.*

It is important for teachers to know and draw upon families' insights into children to connect school and home. Children who struggle with literacy often experience discontinuity between experiences in school and at home. Inviting families to share information and concerns about their children also communicates to families that teachers value parents' perspectives. This is a first step in building trust—and essential for productive partnerships.

2. *Teachers can build bridges of understanding between home and school by a collaborative approach to traditional home–school communications and activities.*

Open school night, parent–teacher conferences, report card day—teachers and families alike view them with trepidation. Too often these events are the only points of contact between family and school. These events are also the moments when teachers and families explicitly address the issues around students' reading issues. We take a closer look at these "taken for granted" events to make explicit the stress points of these established bridges between school and home. Building upon those insights, we propose ways that teachers use school events to collaborate with families to make these events productive as well as to create new events and school traditions, such as literacy walks, game nights, and other interactive occasions to support family involvement in literacy development.

3. *Teachers can build bridges of understanding between home and school by honoring and valuing families' out-of-school literacy experiences as springboards for literacy explorations.*

All families have strengths. Yet struggling readers, experiencing frustrations in school, frequently see themselves as failures. By extension, their families may also focus exclusively on remediating problems. As teachers, we need to cultivate an understanding of the literacy practices that naturally occur within families and helping families support their struggling children.

By listening to families and by providing opportunities to discover the ways families engage in literacy activities, teachers can design and implement experiences for children from this strong base. How literacy exists in families provides teachers the information they need to incorporate children's culture into the curriculum to ensure their academic success, especially for children who struggle with literacy. By beginning instruction from children's strengths and interests, usually identified by the home, teachers have a springboard for developing literacy intervention strategies.

4. *Teachers can build bridges of understanding between home and school by building and expanding on curricular explorations and adapting them to the families' literacy events.*

In partnership with families of children struggling to acquire the literacy needed to be successful in school, teachers can use what they have learned about family literacy to enhance their curriculum efforts. Lowering the drawbridge to allow two sides to connect and ideas to flow to the home of the struggling readers requires teachers to understand the literacy of the home, be creative in ways to communicate with families, and find strategies for families to enhance school learning with activities that do not duplicate those typically found in classrooms. Families of struggling readers often fail to understand how they can be involved in their children's learning. They do not believe the literacy events at home will have any influence on their children's literacy acquisition.

5. *Teachers can build bridges of understanding between home and school by recognizing and celebrating families' cultural diversity through building on the power of storytelling and family stories.*

Storytelling is a fundamental way we share experiences. Through engaging in these oral language activities, literacy development is supported. Struggling readers often possess strengths in oral language that can be utilized to support their growth as readers. Families possess unique individual and cultural storytelling traditions that are often unrecognized and underutilized assets for supporting struggling readers.

This chapter explores the role of oral language and storytelling in the development of literacy skills. We share strategies for teachers to learn about and leverage the oral traditions of their struggling readers and their families.

The stories offered throughout the book are based on our collective experience working with families and students struggling to acquire literacy, but the names used are completely made up. In some cases, we have included direct quotes from actual conversations with those with whom we have worked and have used pseudonyms to protect the original speakers' privacy.

IDEAS TO PONDER

We ask that you consider your own attitudes and current work with families of struggling readers in your classroom. The tool found in appendix 1.1 will help you to identify the areas in which you are knowledgeable, areas in which you may need to up your game, and areas that need your attention.

SUMMARY

This chapter offers the theoretical underpinnings we feel are important and were used to develop the five principles of trust, collaboration, respect, adaptation, and celebration for working with families of struggling readers. Specifically, we reviewed the research supporting the need to make families our literacy partners in working with their children. We defined what we mean when we refer to children who are struggling readers. There are barriers to forming partnerships with families of struggling readers, and we discussed them before offering strategies for working with those families.

Want to Know More?

While the focus of this book is on developing understanding and strategies to form partnerships with families, it's also important to expand your understanding of the multiple ways children struggle with literacy and develop instructional strategies to support them. Here are several places to start:

- Allington, R. L. (2011). *What really matters for struggling readers: Designing research-based programs* (3rd ed.). Boston: Pearson.
- Johnson, P., & Keier, K. (2010). *Catching readers before they fall: Supporting readers who struggle, K–4.* Portland, ME: Stenhouse.
- Vitale-Reilly, P. (2018). *Supporting struggling learners: 50 Instructional moves for the classroom teacher.* Portsmouth, NH: Heinemann.

APPENDIX 1.1

Appendix 1.1 Supporting Families of Struggling Readers: Teacher Self-Assessment

Directions: Please review your own practice and evaluate your *knowledge base* in the following areas/strategies to support families of struggling readers.

	1	2	3	4	5
1: Never tried					
2: Not knowledgeable					
3: Somewhat knowledgeable					
4: Knowledgeable					
5: Very knowledgeable and part of my practice					

1. Use surveys to learn about struggling readers' interests, personality traits, and literacy histories.

2. Use surveys to learn about families' hopes and concerns about their struggling readers' educational experiences.

3. Initiate informal conversations with families at drop-off, pickup, or other school events.

4. Develop and cultivate trust with family members.

5. Demonstrate understanding of diverse family compositions, cultures, and values.

6. Include opportunities to integrate family stories into curriculum.

7. Provide opportunities for families to learn about literacy practices to try at home.

8. Thoughtfully and purposefully plan and implement family literacy events that meet families' needs.

9. Conduct parent–teacher conferences that build on students' literacy strengths.

10. Use accessible language in parent–teacher conferences and in report cards.

11. Effectively communicate with families information about struggling readers' literacy strengths and challenges.

12. Draw on growing knowledge of high-quality children's books to support empathy and understanding of diverse families.

13. Utilize and connect families to community literacy resources.

14. Advocate for families within and outside of schools.

Chapter 2

Evoking Trust by Initiating Conversations

GUIDING PRINCIPLE ONE

Teachers can build literacy bridges of understanding between home and school by initiating trustworthy conversations through surveys and interviews, in order to broaden their understanding of children's literate lives.

Aleja, Emma, Vernados, and Salvador, along with sixteen kindergarten classmates, seated on the classroom carpet, shyly greeted Liz Ishman, their student teacher for the year. Liz knew little of Aleja's fondness for telling jokes, Emma's pride in her mother's recent graduation from community college, Vernados's interest in dinosaurs and the movie *Jurassic Park*, or Salvador's love of basketball.

During this first week, her supervising classroom teacher, Vicki, shared information about the literacy labels already attached to her students through a state-mandated kindergarten readiness test, KRA-L (Kindergarten Readiness Assessment—Literacy [Ohio Department of Education, 2016]), completed in early September. Eight of her twelve Italian, Slovak, African American, Puerto Rican, and Greek five-year-old boys (including Vernados and Salvador) already possessed the testing label of "not on track" readers. None of the eight kindergarten girls, including Aleja and Emma, were labeled struggling readers.

At the onset of her student teaching experience, Liz was quickly introduced to the state-mandated testing profiles of the students; she knew little about their lives outside of the classroom. Growing up in a white, rural community hundreds of miles away, Liz did not yet understand the usefulness of building on diverse families' funds of knowledge or their literate ways with words

(Heath, 1983; Moll, Amanti, Neff, & Gonzalez, 2005). Creating a safe literacy bridge between home and school became one of her key goals.

Labeled a high-needs school located near a diverse urban center, Clairton School District earned a failing grade from their state department of education due to a low graduation rate. Twenty-five percent of Clairton's families lived below the national poverty level. These statistics did not portray the pride Clairton residents displayed when discussing their distinctive suburban community, striving to overcome high poverty and crime rates. Like many educators today, Liz was in the position of teaching more and more ethnically and linguistically diverse children.

She tackled a common cultural and literacy mismatch between white teachers and diverse children by requesting parental input through a family survey, designed to initiate trustworthy conversations. Liz's carefully developed survey is an example of how teachers must take active steps to build literacy bridges with families. Building a literacy bridge designed to span two worlds is not a happenstance but an intentional, negotiated endeavor.

From our work with teachers and parents, we have discovered the importance of recognizing families' contributions to their children's literacy development (Dail & Payne, 2010). The knowledge families possess regarding their children's literacy development cannot be underestimated.

Teachers need a "courageous conviction" (Bildner, 2004) in the midst of uncertainty to muster the courage to cross the literacy bridge and launch conversations. Recognizing this importance led us to the development of our first principle that initiates authentic communication between home and school: *Teachers can build literacy bridges of understanding between*

GUIDING PRINCIPLE ONE

Teachers can build literacy bridges of understanding between home and school by initiating trustworthy conversations through surveys and interviews in order to broaden their understanding of children's literate lives.

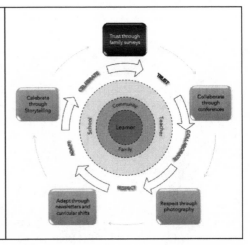

Figure 2.1

home and school by initiating trustworthy conversations through surveys and interviews in order to broaden their understanding of children's literate lives.

INSIGHTS FROM RESEARCH ON FAMILY SURVEYS AND INTERVIEWS

Recognizing Family Instructional Histories

All too frequently, families and teachers see literacy learning as an event exclusive to school (Rowsell, 2006). However, school hours comprise only 25 percent of a child's waking hours during their K–12 experience (Oglan & Elcombe, 2001). Each day during home and community life, family members use multiple literacies, in many unnoticed ways, to decide which movie to watch, to text a friend, to pay bills, or to refill a prescription (Duke & Purcell-Gates, 2003; Goodman, Watson, & Burke, 1996; Harste, 2014). Teachers can use survey and interview questions designed to reveal home literacy practices in order to recognize that children become literate through many different paths.

The use of no-nonsense tools like surveys and family interviews, generating an atmosphere of trust, can jump-start further essential conversations throughout the year (Lawrence-Lightfoot, 2003). Surveys and family interviews consisting of respectful questions can be aimed at recognizing and valuing diverse families' literacy funds of knowledge, a first step for teachers with the goal of helping struggling learners find success at school (Rios-Aguilar, Kiyama, Gravitt, & Moll, 2011).

A critical arena for teachers to tackle consists of exploring their assumptions about parents' instructional literacy histories. Teachers can overcome stereotypes of "deficit" home literacy environments through family surveys by posing respectful, trustworthy literacy questions ("What do you remember about reading in school?" or "When have you caught yourself reading with your child recently? E.g., menus, recipes, road signs, iPhones.").

Family surveys, an indirect form of communication, offer an alternate, less intimidating context for establishing common ground. This less time-consuming option provides busy teachers and families with brief, stolen moments of time (Fleischer, 2000) for initiating yearlong conversations.

A Teacher Mindset for Initiating Conversations

When educators like Liz and Vicki work together with families, children acquire a greater opportunity for experiencing success, particularly struggling readers (Jason, Kuranasaki, Neuson, & Garcia, 1993). Constructing a frame of reference, to help teachers grasp the usefulness of family–school partnerships before offering conversation starters like family surveys or interviews, is a long-term project.

Research on family literacy and family–school partnerships continues to evolve and provide rich evidence of the power of teacher and family collaborations for enhancing student learning (Epstein, 2011; Heath, 2010; Wasik, Dobbins, & Herrmann, 2002). Yet preservice teacher courses and in-service workshops often neglect an adequate focus on building bridges of understanding between teachers and families, school and home, and thereby miss the opportunity to build trust. Without this support, teachers tend to shy away from establishing a strong family–school partnership, particularly when working with diverse parents and families with children who struggle with literacy (Brown, Harris, Jacobson, & Trotti, 2014; Chavkin, 2005; Jensen, 2011).

Some struggling readers like those in Liz and Vicki's classroom come from diverse cultural and linguistic backgrounds. Typically, teachers tend to establish more productive, trusting relationships with families who represent a similar background to their own (Dudley-Marling, 2000). To accept and appreciate difference, an attitudinal change in teachers' frame of reference toward diverse families is required.

Over fifteen years ago, reformist teacher educators such as Geneva Gay (2000) and Gloria Ladson-Billings (1999) highlighted the need within teacher education programs to find avenues for valuing nonmainstream families through culturally responsive pedagogy. Shirley Brice Heath (1983) and Denny Taylor with Catherine Dorsey-Gaines (1988), pioneers in family literacy, began advising teachers to cross the social, cultural, and literacy gap between predominantly white teachers and diverse families and children over twenty-five years ago.

Today, the struggle to connect home with school continues in more complex ways. Teachers must navigate an intense, mandated, standards-based literacy curriculum enforced by annual teacher evaluations, based on demonstrating student literacy growth through test scores. Finding time to work on establishing trustworthy home–school relationships aimed at supporting all readers but especially struggling readers requires a deliberate teacher focus.

Family Interviews to Expand Teachers' Cultural and Literacy Lenses

One-on-one informal interviews with diverse families offer educators an opportunity to build a broader social and literacy lens, a prerequisite when working with struggling readers' families. Through interviews with twenty diverse low-income families, Luet (2015) discovered how "uninvolved" families were in fact quite participatory in undervalued, informal ways such as offering homework support, talking with their children about school regularly, investigating behavioral interventions, talking with teachers when dropping off and picking up children each day, purchasing gifts as rewards for good grades, seeking school advice from friends, encouraging children to learn from their mistakes, monitoring students' technology devices, and volunteering as coaches.

Luet also interviewed these same families' teachers, who narrowly defined parental engagement as attending PTO meetings or parent conferences. When teachers seek to redefine parent participation in terms of families' economic, social, and cultural resources, they can develop a pedagogy built on "the experiences and realities of students' lives" (Campano, 2005, p. 191).

Teachers and preservice teachers benefit from coursework aimed at providing them with opportunities for respecting difference (Chavkin, 2005). For example, during Liz's college sophomore year, she completed a new, state-required preservice teacher course on family–school–community partnerships. A six-week practicum in a Head Start preschool classroom helped Liz witness a school system of early childhood teachers intent on developing strong partnerships with children's first learning partners (Keys, 2014).

Head Start standards outline a clear mandate to educators: "Develop relationships with parents to encourage trust and respectful two-way communication between staff and parents" (Department of Health and Human Services Administration for Children and Families, 2016, p. 43). In a similar way, the International Literacy Association's position statement on family–school partnerships calls for teachers to view family engagement as an integral part of good teaching and student success, while also urging educators to build on families' funds of knowledge (Duke, 2014; International Literacy Association, 2002). Both standards require teachers to become active listeners focused on opening doors to important knowledge about children and their families.

3, 2, 1 STOP AND THINK

3. **Create three** questions for a parent survey or interview that value and respect families' cultural and literate ways of knowing.

2. **Find two** words in your survey or interview that convey trust and a desire to learn from families.

1. **Outline one** goal for using families' ways of knowing in a future learning experience.

BUILDING TRUST FOR FAMILY ENGAGEMENT

As Liz and Vicki demonstrate in our opening story, using family surveys is a powerful first step for initiating literacy conversations. In this section we highlight classroom examples for connecting with families, based on your community's unique social, cultural, and linguistic backgrounds. At the beginning of the year, teachers can reach out through interviews, surveys, or face-to-face conversations, seeking to learn from and embrace students' families, especially those with struggling readers (see figure 2.2 and table 2.1).

"Bold acts of bravery" (Bildner, 2004), in the midst of uncertainty, described the courage required of families with struggling readers invited to cross the literacy bridge into school. Faced with teachers who might not understand or value their cultural and linguistic background, some struggling readers' families chose not to cross the precarious bridge back to school through Liz's survey. They needed attentive teachers determined to bridge the conversation gap. Two parents with children labeled as struggling readers provided vivid insights (see table 2.1).

Brief comments outlining family members' learning-to-read experiences and memories of children's books provided Liz with a starting point for thinking about ways to support parents and grandparents. Family responses for Vernados

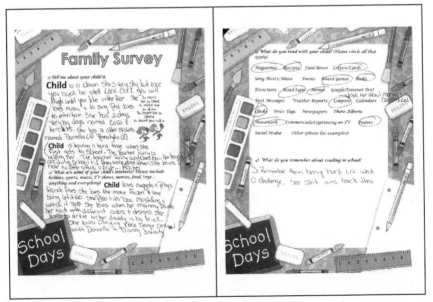

Figure 2.2. Family Survey

Table 2.1. Family Survey Responses

Liz's Family Survey Questions and Families' Responses	
Question 1: Tell me about your child.	Vernados's parent: "Vernados is such a sweet little boy. He's caring, loving, smart, and just enjoys having fun. ... He has a great imagination. He loves playing with his dinosaurs and will play the movie *Jurassic Park*. We read dinosaur books." Salvador's mom: "Salvador can be shy until he feels comfortable. But he is very sweet and loving. ... He plays *Minecraft*, watches SpongeBob, and plays basketball."
Question 4: What do you remember about reading in school?	Vernados's parent: "Hearing the story about that train that could and the story about the elephant who sat on the nest in the tree through bad weather." Salvador's mom: "We were always learning something new, no matter what story we were reading [and] always wondering how it would end."

and Salvador outlined productive memories of specific books from authors like Dr. Seuss and reading as a time of exploration, not a struggle. Typical assumptions teachers hold regarding struggling readers with family members who experienced reading difficulties in school or demonstrated a lack of interest in collaborating with educators did not apply to these families.

Parents' and grandparents' heartfelt observations offered insights into children's social, cultural, and literacy capital. Through the returned surveys, they demonstrated an awareness of school as one crucial place to build self-confidence as well as a space that valued lifelong learning and literacy. Insider information offered by over half of students' first learning partners indicated a willingness to enter into a partnership, thereby supporting Liz's objective of closing the gap between home and school.

This parent survey, seen as an authentic family assessment tool, offered Liz different information from the mandated fifteen-minute analysis of kindergarten learners' ability to manage isolated literacy skills such as identifying capital and lowercase letters, repeating sentences, managing rhyming words, and recognizing initial sounds in English.

In contrast to state testing, the National Council of Teachers of English and the International Literacy Association jointly remind teachers to obtain multiple literacy and family assessments in order to make more informed instructional decisions (NCTE/ILA, 2009). Liz's family survey enabled her to get a window into readers' literate life beyond school, comprising 75 percent of their waking hours each year (Duke & Purcell-Gates, 2003).

As Durán states, "Although many of the skills and resources of working class households and people of color are considered irrelevant to academic learning, teachers attuned to students' funds of knowledge can use them to create powerful contexts for learning" (2016, p. 354). Teachers can design more meaningful activities for children when working collaboratively with parents (Gaitan, 2004).

When educators strive to uncover expectations parents and families hold about their children's literacy development, teachers gain insights for strengthening classroom strategies, activities, and programs. Parents and families possess a wealth of talents and resources that teachers can tap into during the school year. When children see that their teachers and families are working together for their academic success, children begin to value this shared support. The onus for identifying assets families bring to the classroom rests on the teacher's shoulders.

Survey and Interview Language That Builds Trust

Remember to ...
- **Craft** open-ended questions that invite families to describe literacy experiences and their personal literacy capital so that hidden literacy interactions are not devalued (Voss, 1996).
- **Be considerate** of families' diverse—sometimes unsuccessful—experiences at school by creating and celebrating different roles (Gaitan, 2004; Souto-Manning & Swick, 2006).
- **Avoid** overly technical pedagogical language when inquiring about literacy experiences; doing so can act as a subtle, unconscious put-down or microaggression (Compton-Lilly, 2015; Mueller, 2014; Pierce, 1969).

Example	Non-Example
"What do you remember about reading in elementary school?"	*"How many hours do you spend reading stories with your child each week?"*
"Tell me about your child."	*"What words would you use to describe the reading habits of your child?"*
"What are your family's interests?"	*"How often do you visit the library with your child?"*
"What was school like for you at your child's age?"	*"List 3 to 5 of your child's favorite titles."*
"What does your child like to do outside of school?"	

For more trust-building question stems, see the reading interview in Jensen & Tuten (2012).

Teacher Connection

Tamara reflects on talking with families:

It sounds so simple; just get to know the child. Get to know the parents; get to know the children around their parents.

In my orientation, I will say, "Tell me something you want me to know about your child." Parents love to do that, and I'll remember it and bring it up in another conversation, and they will be happy.

Tell me something you really want me to know, and I don't mean allergies, but something positive. You are focusing just on them.

Potentials within Interviews and Surveys

Interviews offer a starting place. We urge teachers to use various forms of informal interviews, even "doorway" conversations, to foster relationships with families. A Title I family literacy night at Foxburg Elementary, a high-needs rural school situated in the nation's Rust Belt, offered a group of twenty-three white preservice teachers an occasion to develop and use open-ended interview questions through conversations with predominantly African American parents and grandparents. Goals for informal interviews conducted over dinner were threefold:

1. Get to know one family or parent by creating personal connections.
2. Inquire about how they strive to stay connected to school.
3. When possible, seek information regarding how they use reading and writing throughout their lives in purposeful ways (Rowsell, 2006).

Taking time to reflect on information shared by family members is pivotal. "Listening to and valuing what parents have to say about their child's learning establishes an effective working relationship between the teacher and the parent" (Herold, 2011, p. 45).

Family surveys offer another opportunity to launch parent literacy conversations. Introductions are a time to uncover children's strengths, not their struggles. The following example demonstrates how a student teacher, Denver, used a letter of introduction sent with the family survey to help families rethink school as the sole place to learn to read (see figure 2.3). Consider how you could adapt this letter to use in your own context.

Denver's words convey a sense of openness to learn from families, the groundwork for establishing a trusting relationship. We believe this open-ended question, "What do you remember about reading in school?" helped Denver and two other student teachers glean these forthright parent responses. The table with the families' words and the teachers' reflections provides enlightening insights (see table 2.2). What might be the responses of the families in your school?

Dear families,

   My name is Miss Baker and I am very excited to begin
working with your student in Ms. Tekac's kindergarten
classroom. As a Westminster College education student, I am
thrilled to begin my practicum experience at Coitsville
Elementary School.

   Kindergarten is such a special year in a child's life. It is the
time where children begin to make sense of the world around
them, as they become young readers. As this moment occurs,
we not only want to encourage the students to read books but
also different things they may see everyday. I would like to
begin thinking about the many different things children may
read daily. This could include items lying around your house,
grocery ads, coupons, signs, family letters, price tags, cereal
boxes, board games, social media, street signs, and much
more!

   I am inviting you to find something your child is reading at
home that is **not a book**, and bring it to school in the bag
attached to the family survey. I know your student is reading
many different things, maybe without even realizing it! ☐

   Thank you for helping us learn more about your child.
Family is a very important part. We can't wait to see the
different things everyone reads at home!

GO RED DEVILS!
       Sincerely,
       Miss Baker

Figure 2.3.   Denver's Introductory Letter

   These family members provide a glimpse into their part-to-whole reading experiences at school ("I can. We can."). They did not view reading as an occasion to comprehend ideas or explore the world (Goodman, 2014). Compton-Lilly (2005) illustrates how "sounding out" can become a cultural model for reading in her study of African American and Puerto Rican families.

   This common reading view, focused on pronouncing high-frequency words accurately (e.g., "I knew I couldn't read well." "I see the apple."), can also be seen in national literacy mandates and standards. In response, teachers can develop a new goal, focused on encouraging family members also to

Table 2.2

Interview Responses and Teacher Reflections	
What Parents Said	What Teachers Learned
"Some things in reading get harder as you get older. All words aren't easy but if you can sound it out, you'll get it." (Kindergarten mom)	"I pushed my stereotypes aside. Chellise's mom told me of her journal with her daughter's teacher so she can keep track of her behavior. She had sent a list of behaviors her daughter might need to work on in school. I was surprised to know that this journal was initiated by the mother. The mother asked the teacher to document Chellise's misbehaviors because she wanted her daughter to learn the discipline plan fast. I actually found myself thinking, 'This sounds like stuff my mom would say.' (Emily)
"Taking turns reading out loud in 1st grade is what I first remember about my childhood and that I didn't want to read and that I knew I couldn't read well and didn't want to be made fun of." (First grade mother)	"I thought these parents would do many things differently than I do but I was wrong. They were very similar to me. They read and write while completing grocery lists, recipes, reminders, job applications, Facebook messages and fundraising orders to name a few. I have written all of these items within the last few weeks." (Molly)
"I see the apple. The apple pik nik park. I can. We can. The alphabet." (Kindergarten parent identified as a struggling reader in elementary school)	"Another way in which Foxborg's families are like mine is seen in a response to my question about how their children see adults reading and writing at home. I remember sitting on my grandfather's lap while he did a crossword puzzle. One of the proudest memories of my life was when I helped my grandpa answer a crossword question. When my Foxborg parent also described a crossword puzzle interaction, I hoped someone else has felt what it is like to sit on grandpa's lap, listening to the rhythms of breath and remembering when they helped grandpa answer a crossword question." (Nick)
In response to the survey question "What do you remember about reading in school?" "I don't remember." "I couldn't read until second grade." "It was a fun experience."	"This survey indicates that either the parent had a terrible experience in reading or that the parent did not find literature he connected to. … This survey stands out to me in many ways. The parent completed the entire survey fully. He also indicated over fifteen ways that he reads with his child including food labels, Internet, price tags, calendars, street signs, cards and jokes. I would like to know more about this family member. I would like to know what he did not like about reading. Something must have changed, as he grew older because he reads to his child a lot. I know this because this child will look at the title of our class story of the day and say, 'My dad read this to me before.' I find it very interesting that this individual did not like reading but incorporates it as part of his daily routine with his child." (Denver)

Table 2.2 *(Cont.)*

Interview Responses and Teacher Reflections	
What Parents Said	*What Teachers Learned*
"It was complicated." "Phonics." "It is a big part of my life."	"This wide range of answers shows me that every parent has a different perspective of literacy and everyone had different experiences when learning to read. … This family literacy survey was an occasion for family members to discuss their own child in terms of his or her early literacy experience. I will keep these 'diverse voices' in mind as I go on to teach; every student [and family member] is going to perceive literacy differently and form a corresponding attitude towards it. … My job is to give them the tools to be excellent readers." (Renee)

Teacher Connection

Kate's use of Remind to communicate with families:

Remind—it's a free app. The parents can download the app themselves, but they don't have to. It's a way for our phone number to stay anonymous, stay in communication, and basically sign them up to a group. It comes to their phone like a regular text message. They can respond like a regular text message, which I know I think everyone likes more than a phone call. … It's quick. If I'm home and a parent asks me a question, it's not a burden for me to text. "No problem, thanks for the heads-up." It's quick and private.

What's even cooler is, on the app, if the parents write to you in Spanish, you can translate it on the app. It's mind-blowing. The language barrier with one parent was tough, but with the app we could translate it right there.

What I love even more is you can send pictures, even when we go on field trips. You know not every parent can go, so if I have a really cute picture of a kid on the bus I'm going to send it right then. It gives them some positive stuff.

Other ways teachers can use technology to survey families include the following:

- Google Forms: https://docs.google.com/forms
- SurveyMonkey: https://www.surveymonkey.com/
- Polldaddy: https://polldaddy.com/

---

recognize the value of comprehension, a natural component when families and children read everyday texts like street signs, calendars, or text messages. The importance of this strategy, in particular to support struggling readers at home, will be addressed in detail in chapter 4.

Collecting parent feedback is getting easier through social media. Teachers can harness digital tools, available in multiple languages, to learn from families. Sites such as SurveyMonkey or Google Forms can help teachers create free online surveys for families to complete on their phones, tablets, or computers. Including open-ended questions such as "Tell me about your child" and "What does your family enjoy doing on the weekend?" as well as multiple-choice, Likert-scale types of prompts communicates a teacher's interest in learning more about her students, as well as provides concrete information to guide and enrich instruction.

The prolific use of iPhones and apps helps teachers find simple ways to obtain survey feedback quickly.

Highlighting Literacy Successes

Like the two sides of a bridge, "The crux of communication rests on the willingness of both sides to listen to the other's position and negotiate" (Gaitan, 2004, p. 23). The role of teacher as listener provides a new path for building trusting home–school bridges via family interviews and surveys. Thoughtful listeners recognize the need to respond and build on families' social, cultural, and literacy insights, by showing parents how literacy learning is a shared responsibility between families and educators. It is critical, once teachers elicit this information, to acknowledge and honor the time and attention families have invested in sharing this information, and to view it as an asset.

Trustworthy home–school relationships need to explore both the literacy successes and difficulties all readers naturally encounter. The families we learned with shared numerous literacy successes through interviews and reveal some reading strengths and struggles through surveys. Both home–school conversations offered different potentials for establishing a trustworthy bridge of understanding across readers' two unique literacy communities. When teachers choose to focus conversations on literacy successes first, before tackling struggling readers' difficulties, they establish a respectful tone for conversations with children's first learning partners. Parents benefit from hearing teachers highlighting what is working first, a frequently overlooked aspect of developing meaningful relationships.

The families we described thus far, most with children who struggle in reading, revealed a wealth of literacy successes through family interviews and surveys, evident in their everyday literacy interactions (Rowsell, 2006; Street, 2001). Teachers can uncover and capitalize on literacy engagements meant to sustain lifelong learning for children and families.

"Learning how literacy exists in households is important for educators, particularly teachers. With knowledge of children's home life, teachers can incorporate the children's culture into the curriculum and build a stronger foundation for their academic success" (Gaitan, 2004, p. 8). With information from interviews and surveys, teachers are in a position to use families' funds of knowledge to make informed curricular decisions like selecting a

Table 2.3

Ways of Responding to Understandings Gained through Surveys and Interviews *How can teachers honor families' voices?*	
Maintaining momentum through dialogues (report cards, thank-you letters) about student growth	**Chapter 3**: Reimagining Collaborative School–Home Events
Capturing home literacy experiences through photography	**Chapter 4**: Generating Respect for Home and Community Literacy Experiences
Reflecting families' interests and expertise through curricular adaptations and home–school literacy projects (newsletters)	**Chapter 5**: Adapting Curriculum to Include Families' Ways of Knowing
Celebrating families' traditions and cultures through multimodal storytelling (blogs, literacy nights)	**Chapter 6**: Celebrating Literacy through Sharing Stories

wider variety of books for independent reading time at school and, for inclusion in home–school book bags, creating reading bookmarks designed to offer students and their families multiple strategies for tackling new words and ideas.

We circle back to Liz, whose partnership with Clairton families introduced this chapter. She provides further evidence of her desire to listen to the voices of overlooked literacy partners at the close of student teaching in this way: "You really learn to value what the families have at home and to see the way that [each] child views learning, reading, and the world in general. It's giving parents a say in their child's education and helping the teacher to make all kinds of decisions based off of information about their students, not just based off standards."

Readers who face literacy difficulties require strong partnerships attentive to generating trust, an essential element for building bridges (McGrath, 2014). Bridges built to cross home–school chasms need to be carefully maintained. Providing trustworthy conversation spaces through family interviews and surveys followed by notes of thanks and newsletters can be seen as the first step toward building a systemic and sustainable framework for family literacy engagement (Weiss, Lopez, & Rosenberg, 2010). Applicable to all schools, family interviews and surveys provide teachers with an initial step aimed at facilitating further literacy conversations.

When schools recognize the need to develop robust parent–school partnerships for families whose children struggle with reading, they deliberately focus professional development on expanding teachers' sociocultural lens on literacy learning (Dudley-Marling, 2009). As teachers recognize their responsibility to initiate conversations designed to listen and respond to families' diverse social, cultural, and literacy perspectives, they demonstrate their trustworthiness to families with struggling readers, an initial step necessary for creating a safe crossing between home and school.

Learning to embrace and listen to families takes time and practice. Liz and Vicki, along with other teachers, offer vital demonstrations. Families with struggling readers seize opportunities to share their child's strengths as teachers demonstrate their "courageous conviction" to listen (Bildner, 2004). Surveys and interviews create openings for reluctant parents to become receptive to future conversations between home and school.

SUMMARY

To create trust with families, rethink typical questions used in surveys and interviews so as not to create a chasm between home and school. Offer family members time to share their strengths through surveys and interviews, and struggles if they feel comfortable. Respond to family literacy information through thank-you notes and newsletters, demonstrating the usefulness of their literacy funds of knowledge.

Want to Know More?

- Explore diverse home lives and family practices in Annette Lareau's (2003) *Unequal Childhoods: Class, Race, and Family Life.*
- Review Elsa Auerbach's (1995) "Deconstructing the Discourse of Strengths in Family Literacy," *Journal of Reading Behavior,* to learn more about the role language plays in consideration of children's literacy development.
- Explore Denny Taylor and Catherine Dorsey-Gaines's (1988) *Growing Up Literate* to read about families in an urban context.
- Browse Gloria Ladson-Billings's (1999) "Preparing Teachers for Diverse Student Populations: A Critical Race Theory Perspective," *Review of Research in Education,* for deeper discussion of the role of race in teacher preparation.
- Examine Patricia Edwards and colleagues' (1999) *A Path to Follow* to learn more about ways to learn from parents' stories.

CHILDREN'S BOOKS

Dominguez, M., & Lombana, J. (2014). *El chavo: El partido de futbol/The soccer match.* New York: Scholastic.

Parr, T. (2010). *The family book.* New York: Little, Brown.

Chapter 3

Reimagining Collaborative School–Home Events

GUIDING PRINCIPLE TWO

Teachers can build bridges of understanding between home and school by a collaborative approach to traditional home–school communications and activities.

On a cold Tuesday evening, Denise Johnson sat on a small, child-sized chair outside her son Jayson's third grade classroom. She had switched shifts at her job at the city's sanitation department so that she could attend the first parent–teacher conference of the year. Attending parent–teacher conferences has always been a priority, and this year Denise was particularly anxious to meet with Jayson's teacher.

Denise has noticed that it is getting harder for Jayson to complete his homework, especially his 30 minutes of reading and writing in his reading log. He would stay at the table for a few minutes, then get up, roam around, doodle cartoon characters on the paper, anything but read. Denise believed he was smart—too smart sometimes for his own good—but hated to read and write. She has heard that the test this year is important and that the reading portion was hard and the writing portion even harder. His teacher last year told her he's a good talker but, as school gets harder, he will need other skills in order to be successful.

As the time passed by, Denise grew more anxious about the conference. Suddenly, thoughts of her own school experiences raced into her mind. Denise still lived in the neighborhood she grew up in, a large northeastern city. Predominantly African American and working class, it was an area in flux. While Denise still lived in the home she grew up in, there had been a recent push toward gentrification.

While she loved school when she was in elementary, she struggled in middle school when her mom got very sick. High school became a social relief from home, and she didn't want to go to college. Maybe if she'd continued with school, she thinks, she would be a better mom. What will she learn about Jayson's reading and writing? What more can she do to help? Denise wondered, "Is it my fault he's struggling?"

Inside the classroom, Jessica Anderson, a second-year teacher and a new third grade teacher in a large urban school, was also anxious about the upcoming conferences. That year there were twenty-nine students in the classroom. Already now in November, she struggled to keep on top of curriculum, the variety of school initiatives, and her own evening graduate courses. As an untenured teacher, she was concerned about her own performance.

Many of her students were struggling in reading. Some of them were good decoders but had limited comprehension skills; others couldn't translate ideas into writing, or their reading levels were below expected. Part of her teacher evaluation was based on moving her struggling readers to higher benchmark levels. Her school didn't have a literacy coach; going to her principal for help, she'd been advised by peers, would be seen as a sign of weakness.

Jayson was one of her struggling students. According to her running record assessment, he scored well below the expected grade level. Yet when she worked with him one-on-one or in a small group, he offered interesting comments and insight; he made steady progress. She observed how much he likes to draw and his great skill in drawing funny cartoons, including thought bubbles. However, in other contexts, he could be very disruptive and impatient.

Additionally, he didn't fully complete his homework. Jessica was not really sure how to help Jayson. With all the different curricula to cover, there wasn't time to give him the individual attention she knew made a difference. She had to admit this was professionally and personally upsetting. As she prepared for the parent–teacher conference, she wondered how she could discuss her concerns about Jayson without showing her frustration.

As one can see from the story, parents and teachers are deeply invested in supporting children who struggle with reading, but they are both often unsure when they meet how to achieve their goals, coming as they do from different perspectives. But if they work together as a team, they can achieve what may seem unimaginable.

As we previously discussed with the first principle, sharing knowledge, developing curricular connections between home and school, and increasing communication channels are all critical in building literacy bridges. Through this second principle, we look carefully at the well-established, traditional school "genres" of home–school connections, such as parent–teacher

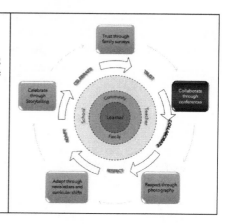

Figure 3.1

conferences and report cards. Our second principles states: *Teachers can build bridges of understanding between home and school by a collaborative approach to traditional home–school communications and activities.*

INSIGHTS FROM RESEARCH ABOUT FAMILY–SCHOOL COMMUNICATIONS

Family Knowledge

One of the problems that families experience, especially families of struggling students, is the competing views of their students, as discussed earlier in chapters 1 and 2. Teachers, more and more, do not share the cultural or racial backgrounds of their children and can struggle to understand the points of view and experiences of families different from them.

Because of this gap, teachers may also develop a deficit perspective and fail to recognize family strengths (for further discussion, see chapter 4). Additionally, with increased focus on accountability measures at the local, state, and national levels, teachers are focused on academic performance. This narrowed focus, especially when students are not making progress in traditionally measurable ways, can misguidedly lead teachers (and administrators) to look for causes of failure.

Unfortunately, many teachers blame families. Anna, a second grade teacher in an urban school states, "If the parents don't read to them or help with the homework, what am I supposed to do?" Her frustration continues when only four or five parents show up for her September open school night. "I had put all this work into making packets and a slide show, and I was kind of annoyed that they didn't care enough to show up." Comments like this demonstrate the deficit views teachers unfortunately hold about the families in their schools.

Parents, too, come to school meetings and events with complex experiences, perspectives, and needs. Linguistic, educational, and cultural differences may feel insurmountable. Work and child-care schedules may be incompatible with school-centric calendars.

And so family members like Denise Johnson may see strengths in students in outside-of-school activities and be confused or angry when a teacher states, through a report card or a parent–teacher meeting, that their son or daughter is struggling. For example, White (2009) discussed what she calls the public school narrative "that disadvantage is compensatory. It suggests that remedial reading programs ... should fix the problems and make children do better in school" (p. 431). Yet she discovers through listening to mothers' stories that mothers often have a unique lens on their children's learning.

White (2009) shares the story of Betty, whose son Paul was labeled a struggling reader in second grade. However, what becomes apparent is that Paul was disinterested in the primarily fairy tales and imaginary stories presented as part of the curriculum. "Betty had a solid knowledge of her son as a literacy learner, but it did not match institutional knowledge. Her story helps us to see that parents who do not come to school are not necessarily staying away because they do not care or do not want to participate" (p. 431). From Betty, White learns the importance of eliciting information about children from families at conferences and meetings.

Similarly, Whitmore and Norton-Meier (2008) present two case studies of mothers in a rural area, one who is on public assistance and the other who is working class, and shared that "in both homes, adults and children used oral and written language to remember, create, express emotion, document, figure out, investigate, and relate to one another" (p. 459). However, each family had a child that was seen by the school as struggling.

Both women, with interrupted or limited schooling, were distrustful of their own abilities to help their child but valued school success. When invited to participate in meaningful school activities, their unique contributions were recognized and valued. "Pearl, in the role as expert author, and Rhonda, during a special food event for teachers, became more confident and comfortable when their talents were validated and given a place of importance and respect in the school culture" (p. 460).

Difficult Conversations in Parent–Teacher Conferences

In her classic book *The Essential Conversation* (2003), Sara Lawrence-Lightfoot describes the complicated and emotionally fraught dynamics of the parent–teacher conference. She advises,

The conference must not be reduced to a reporting out of test scores and a recounting of innocuous platitudes. Rather, there must be a stance of welcoming parents, seeking their alliance, listening to their perspectives, honoring the ways in which they see and know their child, and seeing them as a valuable and essential resource for working successfully with their children. This stance of alliance rather than competition, of bridge building rather than boundary drawing, must not be seen as a distraction from teaching and learning—the central agenda of school—rather, it must be seen as a necessary dimension of building successful relationships with children that will ultimately support their academic success. (p. 237)

As we explored earlier, mother Denise Johnson and teacher Jessica Anderson each have special and unique knowledge about Jayson, and each care deeply about creating pathways for his success.

Stevens and Tollafield (2003) assert, "Parent conferences should be models of good communication, integrally involving parents in their child's education" (p. 521). They outline a checklist featuring ten considerations to support schools in creating "a positive climate that enhances the conference process for parents and teachers," including invitation techniques, ideas for safe atmospheres, information selection tips, and communication reflection questions (p. 521).

Parents' ability to actively participate in meetings can be affected by an imbalance of power between families and school professionals (Mueller, 2014). Howard and Lipinoga (2010) investigate misunderstandings between parents and teachers as a result of inattention to linguistic and cultural differences. As they examine the experiences of Mexican immigrant families at parent–teacher conferences, they find that families did not feel welcome. "This feeling among parents was likely influenced by the fact that teachers very rarely engaged in rapport-building activities such as greetings with Spanish-speaking parents, leaving this to the interpreters" (p. 40). They suggest, "Teachers are able to build rapport with English-speaking parents through greetings and small talk, and they explain the curriculum in terms that are more accessible to these parents: These same practices could be brought to conferences with Spanish-speaking parents" (p. 44).

There is a growing awareness and attention to the preparation of teachers to engage with families. Yet very few teacher preparation programs explicitly address practices such as composing report cards or leading parent–teacher conferences. Kroeger and Lash (2011), looking at teacher preparation ways of introducing family engagement to preservice teachers, discover "school people and accrediting bodies may state they value family involvement but how to actualize that value seems to escape many schools and teachers" (p. 271); they argue, "In order to support families, to be respectful and to allow parents to have a voice in schools, a teacher must grow comfortable with becoming close to parents, and entering communities that fall beyond their common experience" (p. 271).

In a study using simulated parent–teacher conferences, Dotger, Harris, Maher, and Hansel (2011) find that teachers lacked awareness about how issues of "race, class, gender, familial structure, dis/ability, inclusion, and religion are manifest within classroom contexts" (p. 809). To be able to effectively and, most importantly, authentically build bridges with families in the context of parent–teacher conferences, teachers must develop heightened understanding and sensitivities:

> Professional dialogue begins with teachers' awareness of, and sensitivity to, the diverse racial, ethnic, socioeconomic, cultural, and disability demographics of students and their families. Based on this foundation of awareness and sensitivity, teachers are limited only by the degree to which they possess the skill sets to engage in productive dialogue with parents and caregivers, their primary allies in the support of student success. (p. 805)

Lawrence-Lightfoot, too, would argue that teachers benefit from exposure and experiences to engage parents so that they enter into the parent–teacher conference with an open and productive stance toward families, much like this research reveals. Teachers with whom we have worked echo the sentiments of teachers in Dotger, Harris, Maher, and Hansel's (2011) study, as they "stress the importance and sensitivity to compromise, the danger of assumptions, the complexities of parent-student relationships, and the complexities of teacher-parent conversations" (p. 810).

In their work with Latino families, Lopez and colleagues (2005) suggest that information presented to families must be both clear and concise and should be in the preferred language and communication mode of the family. This is especially true for families of students who are struggling with literacy acquisition.

Teacher/Parent Connection

Melissa (a teacher and parent of a struggling reader) shares her insights

Every report card meeting that I have with a parent of a child struggling, I see struggling in the same way I saw Maria [her daughter] struggle. I speak to the parents; I see the looks on their faces. Right away, the first thing I want to do is say is,"It's not your fault. You didn't do anything wrong. You couldn't have known," and I give them my perspective of being a parent of a struggling reader.

Dilemmas of Report Cards

Since the nineteenth century, report cards have been a staple summative evaluation in U.S. schools. Gursky (2002) identifies six general dimensions educators and researchers note for the purposes of report cards: communication of achievement to parents and others, information to help students understand their own progress, identification and selection of students for courses or programs, evaluation of instructional programs, and evidence of students' effort or responsibility. With these justifications, teachers and families alike often find the report card itself a challenging experience. Teachers find it difficult to put all they know and care about regarding students into a form (Afflerbach & Johnston, 1993; Lomax, 1996; Lyons, 1990), and standardized language distances families from understanding the strengths and complexity of their children (Comber, 1996; Tuten, 2007).

When we look at how report cards communicate literacy performance, there is a tendency for them to reduce reading to a number (Afflerbach, 2017; Tuten, 2007). Report cards typically do not document the literacy assessment and teaching practices of schools and so provide families with narrow and limited information about a child's progress and challenges.

In fact, categories and evaluation systems often do not align with school curricula, and "most schools persist in using reporting forms that are poorly aligned, inadequate, and ineffective" (Swan, Gurskey, & Jung, 2014, p. 291). Moreover, language used in report cards is geared toward educators not families. It fails to give families information about school expectations and does not invite families to share their own perspective (Block et. al. 2009). Further, Block and colleagues (2009), after analyzing report cards from across the country, argue that report cards do not build home–school connections—they are one-way streets: "For instance, present report cards do not enable caregivers to give feedback about (a) what or how much a child has transferred literacy abilities to out-of-school settings, (b) how teachers can advance the learning process for their child from their perspective, and (c) how to improve the information that was reported" (p. 37). In most areas, current report card forms fail to meet the needs of ESL students and students with special needs. Report cards typically highlight deficits and fail to explicitly acknowledge and address assets, which is so important for families of struggling readers to know.

Munk and Bursuck (2001) surveyed parents about how well report cards described the literacy achievement of their children and found a gap in perceptions between parents of high-achieving students and those who had learning issues. They found that "parents of students with disabilities commented that grades did not reflect their child's effort or progress and did not describe the specific strengths of their students" (p. 285).

Programs to "Teach" or "Train" Families

Because of the Federal requirements of No Child Left Behind, and currently Every Student Succeeds Act (ESSA), many schools and districts put into place family literacy programs. While well intentioned, without careful and strategic planning these kinds of programs may not authentically reach families.

Typically, these programs are school directed, and the agenda is set by school needs (Baird, 2015). They focus on observable, measurable practices such as parent–teacher conferences, back-to-school nights, and PTO meetings (Jeynes, 2010). These kinds of practices may not adequately address the needs of families nor allow parents to have a voice in setting the agenda. Practices such as these reinforce the power positions within a school, placing parents as outsiders with limited decision-making roles despite their deeply held need within the educational process.

Reese, Sparks, and Leyva (2010) reviewed experimental studies of parent interventions for preschool children's language and emergent literacy and categorized three primary types of interventions: parent–child book reading, parent–child conversations, and parent–child writing. While all programs reviewed demonstrated impact on children's development, they found that different programs create different results and cautioned that all programs may not meet the specific contextual and cultural needs of a group of families.

For example, most studies of parent–child book reading found that the existing programs were not as effective for children of low-income families. "If we want to reach beyond middle-class populations with effective interventions for their language skills, then we need to know more about cultural differences in the role of books in the home and how parents structure shared reading with their children" (Reese, Sparks, & Leyva, 2010, p. 108). They argue for more attention to "building onto home literacy practices ... rather than merely superimposing styles of talk that have been shown to be beneficial to children from middle-class models of intervention" (p. 108).

Counterexamples recognize the complexity in developing a mutually beneficial family literacy program. Barone (2011) argues that successful programs recognize and work on the misconceptions that teachers have about families and the complicated feelings families may have about schools. She describes a successful program that focused on supporting shared reading at home, emphasizing the importance of recruiting community parents to become facilitators and leaders as trust was fostered between home and school.

It was also important to create experiences for family members to observe literacy practices and try them out with the support of teachers so that they feel confident trying them out at home. Similarly, Lam and colleagues (2013) worked with preschool families to learn and enact a single reading strategy and found that the effects of that strategic support increased not only the reading achievement of the children but the parents' sense of efficacy as well. Parents were instructed in reading in pairs with their children and in providing targeted feedback, but with a clear focus on enjoying the reading activity; doing so "gets children some peaceful private attention from their parents. In addition, the procedure gives parents a clear, straightforward, and enjoyable way of helping their children" (p. 127). Further, Lam and colleagues argue,

> At the end of the program they had higher self-efficacy in helping their children to be better readers. Nevertheless, the increase in self-efficacy was not only restricted to helping their children to read, but was generalized to helping their children to be better learners. The program had empowered the parents in their parenting skills and abilities. They were more confident in using praise and encouragement in a timely manner and did so readily to reinforce their children's learning in general. (p. 133)

Along with specific programs are family literacy nights. These are often one- or two-night events. Some programs are designed exclusively for parents and focus on informing or "training" parents in an aspect of reading development or instruction. Other programs invite parents and children to attend together in shared activities or events that promote reading and writing. But strategies offered at family literacy nights should be applicable to families with struggling readers.

There are also parallel programs in which parents and children each attend a workshop and then meet at the end to share what was learned. In a recent study, Dennis and Margarella (2017) reported that family literacy nights generate positive responses from both families and children, but they provide some caution given that families who attend are often enthusiastic, good readers. They suggest that schools make stronger and more focused efforts to connect with families of struggling readers to bring them to such events. They also urge family representation in planning such events.

It is also key to remember that family literacy nights, specific programs or workshops to "train" or instruct families, and parent–teacher conferences are all physical facets of involvements. As discussed earlier, only viewing parental involvement as "showing up" may exclude or deter partnerships for a variety of reasons.

For example, Epstein (2001) created a framework that defines parental involvement behaviors as parenting, communicating, volunteering, learning at home, decision making, and collaborating with the community (p. 121). However, assumptions are made about the perspectives and abilities of families. Hong (2011) challenges the model of family engagement that "centers on schools, promotes activities, views parents as deficits, limits participation, and alters parenting practices" (p. 26). She argues for an ecological model of parent engagement that "centers on parents, promotes engagement, views parents as assets, broadens participation, and transforms families, schools, and communities" (p. 26).

Similarly, Poza and colleagues (2014) discuss the barriers to coming to school, which include language, time, lack of resources, sense of not being welcome, and perceptions of bias from school (p. 143). Workshops can be videotaped and made available for family members whose schedules prevent them from attending. Any handouts could be posted online for families to download and have.

Challenges of Special Education

For many families, there is an undercurrent of concern when teachers raise issues, in parent–teacher meetings and through report card evaluations, that these messages may be a precursor to a special education evaluation or diagnosis. "The U.S. special education system is saturated with technical and cultural conventions that make parental navigation extremely difficult" (Mueller, 2014, p. 4). An Individualized Educational Plan (IEP) results in a unique document that contains assessment information, much like a report card, and instructional goals. It also creates a diagnosis or label that, for many families, can be a complex experience.

Most importantly, an IEP is also a contract, with legal status, that informs the commitments of the school to the education of the child. Taylor (1991) powerfully describes the struggles of a family as they journey through the special education assessment process. She documents the disparities and contradictions between the prescribed testing measures and her own assessments of a young reader, Patrick. Taylor argues that school-mandated tests and assessments accrue too great authority to drive placement and service decisions, to the exclusion of other voices, such as family, which can result in denial of authentic learning opportunities. Mehan (1996) questions the referral system, which may start with a teacher's request for help with a puzzling student but can become removed from the student and context, making the student into an object. He finds that in the IEP meeting, the perspectives of the school psychologist, who often meets the student only once, is privileged over the views of the parents and the classroom teacher.

Even when a parent is more forthright and articulates the strengths of her child, the results of a committee on special education (CSE) meeting to discuss an IEP may run counter to the expressed desires of a student and her family. Rogers (2002) used critical discourse analysis to examine CSE meetings involving a teen. Examining the transcripts of the two meetings, along with other data such as interviews, participant observations, and archival data, Rogers found tensions in how power relationships were enacted in the language used to discuss the student. In her analysis, she found great complexity in the discourse used to construct the teen:

Alleged deficits that were severe enough to label Vicky as "multiply disabled" became her strengths. However, the logic of the process did not operate by telling the child and her parents that the child was not doing well in the self-contained classroom but that she was thriving. Thus, it appeared as if the child flourished in the self-contained classroom, confirming the placement as an educational decision. Further, although the evidence to get a child classified demanded standardized test scores and a number of official representatives of the school, there was no evidence provided in order to get Vicky removed from special education. (p. 6)

In CSE meetings, much like in parent–teacher conferences, families' voices are frequently silenced or limited.

Yet as difficult and fraught as the special education evaluation process may be, the access and affordances that may support a child's literacy growth can be present there. The possibility of referral is often first broached by a classroom teacher, and these discussions heighten the already high-stakes nature of the parent–teacher conference. Rachel, a third grade teacher at a charter school, related how difficult it was to share her concerns about a student's difficulties with language development. When the parents did not give consent for an evaluation, she felt frustrated.

Parent Connection

Bari shares the story of her son's experience with a school's evaluation process

When my son was in the third grade, early in the third grade, the teacher mentioned he was struggling in the class. So I made an appointment to meet with her and the assistant principal.

But when we were sitting there, the teacher didn't say anything, not that she recommended that we meet or that she felt my son was struggling. I made the assistant principal aware of the teacher's observation, and he said, "Well, I don't think the Board of Ed will do anything about it since he's only reading one letter away from where he should be." Again, the teacher just sat there and didn't say anything. If she had said something, that she believed he was struggling, or pushed to get him evaluated, I would have had a better idea of the direction to take. Based on her initial conversation with me, I did what I had to do: I made the appointment, I sat with them, and then they are telling me there's nothing they can do. If the teacher was more involved with my son and saw that he was struggling, she should be able to say something to whoever is in charge, the principal or assistant principal, and make a recommendation. But that teacher didn't say anything. Maybe if she had said something it would have been different.

So he took the [the third grade state]test. He failed with a score of 199, and apparently 200 was the required passing score. So they said he failed the grade. I tried to make an appointment with the principal. I was told there was nothing they could do. He had to stay back.

3, 2, 1 STOP AND THINK

---

3. **List three** challenges you face when thinking about family–school communication.
2. **Recall two** successful moments of family–school communication in your class room or school. What made these moments successful?
1. **Create one** next step for fostering your communication with families.

COLLABORATION FOR FAMILY ENGAGEMENT

In the opening of this chapter, we encountered Denise Johnson and Jessica Anderson on opposite sides of the classroom door, both with mixed feelings of eagerness and apprehension. Was a real discussion possible? Both women bring to the meeting an "essential conversation" (Lawrence-Lightfoot, 2003), their educational histories and experiences; Jayson remains at the center of the conversation, a unique nine-year-old boy. Jessica opens the conversation as she greets Denise at the door and ushers her into the classroom:

> *Jessica:* Thank you for coming tonight. I'm looking forward to learning about Jayson from you and sharing what we've been working on this year. Let me tell you about an amazing conversation I had with him the other day after our class discussion about friendship. ...

By opening the conference with an invitation to share her own insights and then telling a positive story, Jessica takes steps to lay a positive groundwork to a conversation about Jayson's strengths and needs. She next invites Denise to share her concerns:

> *Denise:* Well, I am kind of wondering about this test coming up. I'm not exactly clear on what he needs to do and I try to get Jayson to get on with his homework, but sometimes I just can't help. Is he going pass?
>
> *Jessica:* I see. Let me show you how I've learned about Jayson's reading. He reads aloud a passage, and I write down what he reads and then ask him some questions. I find that he reads really fast and skips over words or sometimes says something that doesn't quite make sense. Then he can answer some questions and find answers in the book but has trouble thinking about what he has read. For the test, he will need to read more slowly and carefully, and some of the answers to the questions aren't right there in the text but need his good thinking. That's why I give homework. But maybe we can look at it together to see if we can make some changes that will work for everyone.

In this conversation, Jessica invites Denise to share her concerns and validates her response. She shares what she notices about his reading in accessible lan- guage, not teacher jargon. Doing this assures Denise of Jessica's knowledge and close attention to her son's reading practices. It also provides a peek at the

Table 3.1. Literacy Jargon Translation

"Teacher" Term	*"Family" Term*
Comprehension	*Understanding what we read*
Phonics/Decoding	*Breaking down the word into parts*
Inferencing	*Connecting beyond the text to make deeper meaning*
Strategies	*Tools that help us make meaning*
Fluency	*Reading out loud without stopping often to break down words*

reading process. Jessica also explains her rationale behind the homework that has proven to be a struggle and invites Denise to partner with her to develop solutions. Table 3.1 provides a brief "translation" guide.

Building Trust

As we learned from the experiences of Liz and her colleagues in chapter 2, and considering the first principle, the beginnings of building trust occur when we use nonjudgmental beginning-of-the-year surveys to get to know families. With this foundation, school-based events like parent–teacher conferences can become less stressful and more meaningful.

Barone (2011) posits that building trust between families and school is the essential first step before implementing any authentic literacy collaboration. In her project, a bilingual story reading series of engagements, she first elicited from families what they wanted and needed to know. It was planning with the families in mind, not the convenience and needs of the teachers and the school.

Providing useful information formats that are accessible is essential. Allen (2007) suggests reaching out to bilingual families in several ways. Teachers who don't speak the same languages as their students and families can recruit a family liaison to contact families about events. Regular parent breakfasts with teachers and leaders can become a space for families to share their feelings about how school can support their struggling students. Use "Communicating with Families: A Self-Assessment" at the end of this chapter (appendix 3.1) to reflect on the ways you currently communicate with families and set goals for further action.

Reimagined Report Cards

While report card formats are frequently determined without direct teacher input or advice, there are strategies teachers can use to address some of the challenges report cards create for teacher and families alike. Tuten (2007) suggests the tips in textbox 3.1.

Textbox 3.1 Reimagined Report Cards

---

1. Recognize and welcome the range of family members that may have caregiving roles in students' lives.
2. Be sure to ask parents about children's strengths in meetings: "Tell me what your child does well," or "Tell me what your child does that makes you smile."
3. Labels such as "shy" or "disruptive" or "slow" may have negative interpretations. Describe rather than label in report cards and in conferences.
4. Support families in understanding the school's assessment system. Consider creating a jargon-free guide to accompany report cards with your colleagues.
5. Advocate for resources, such as translators, child care, or refreshments, so that families can comfortably participate in conferences.
6. When possible, become involved with administration or district leadership to develop reporting formats that align with your beliefs and practices about literacy learning but that also maintain consistency and accountability.

Here is an example of teachers who have taken the last step. When a new report card form was introduced, a group of fourth grade teachers at an urban school were not happy. They wrote a letter to the families: "The short form [issued by their large district] was meant to improve on the impossibly long form of the previous year, but the fourth grade teachers felt that the short form did not accurately reflect the teaching that we do at our school. So we modified an upper-grade report we have used in the past. We hope it is helpful." The form the teachers adapted included many specific literacy practices that the teachers were addressing in their instruction. For example, the official report card indicators for Reading were "Reads independently for sustained periods of time," "Reads aloud fluently," and "Shows evidence of understanding text." The teachers' revised report card tripled the number of indicators to include more descriptive and concrete reading behaviors, such as "Selects books that match reading level and interests" and "Participates in read-aloud conversations."

Finally, the teachers tried to create a supportive context for families and children to understand and use the information within the report card: "We have done our best to give grades based on a careful look at each individual child, and I hope that the report will help you and your child identify areas of strength and areas that need improvement as we continue through the year. Please praise your child for any good grades, and we will work hard to improve in areas that are a problem for him or her." For families of children who struggle, this message helps contextualize the report card. It invites the family to participate in supporting the student.

More Productive Parent–Teacher Conversations

"I hoped teachers would inform me between conferences if anything was amiss or pleasing about my children's progress, socially or academically, so that there would be no big surprises during the conferences" (McCarthy, 2015). Parent–teacher conferences can be more productive if they are not the first time families and teachers are meeting. McCarthy (2015) suggests having at least two or three personal contacts or connections prior to the conference. While most schools designate specific days and times for conferences, the intense scheduling and pace of holding twenty to thirty conferences in a short period of time is not conducive to meaningful discussions. If conferences are held as needed and scheduled *with* families not *for* families, it already sets a different tone.

McCarthy (2015) suggests the following team-building strategies within the conference. First, lead with areas of progress or observed strengths. Second, accurately inform families about need along with the steps the teacher will be taking. This can reassure families that the teacher is knowledgeable and proactive. Finally, make one concrete suggestion that is appropriate for families to do to support their child (see chapter 5 for further ideas). Here are some parent views:

> I want the teacher to start by telling me something my kid did right. Then I'd like her or him to ask, "What questions do you have?"

> I want evidence that the teacher has put together a thoughtful plan for meeting the needs of my child, and it is one that he or she can articulate and provide evidence for how it is being implemented.

Another way for the parent–teacher conference to be transformed is to include the student. More and more schools implement student-led conferences (Bailey & Gurskey, 2000). With this format, the student is not only present but an active participant, and the focus can be on student work, with exemplars or portfolios serving as the focal point. Frank, a middle school English teacher, reflects:

> I think that student-led conferences are really effective. We do a lot of portfolio-based assessments, so students have a plethora of their work that they can discuss. I think that through that as a conduit and that is going to bridge the gap. [*sic*] I also feel that parents often hear teachers say a lot of things and sometimes there's a disconnect and sometimes it's a more powerful thing when a student is obviously the most important thing because he or she is doing the work. They bring us together. So I think student centered is much more appropriate.

Teacher Connection

Kate shares her use of progress folders to foster ongoing communication with families:

As a team, we created Progress Folders. They are sent home three times a year. There are three sections. The first one has home activities. So the first time it has things like, my "at home goals" is practicing the letters I don't know, the sounds that I don't know, but by the next one they commonly get their gold ticket like, "I can do all my letters." Then there are sight words, and the last one there are sight words and reading strategies, and there's data there. So we sit with every child and fill them out and then go into the folder. The next pocket has the resources, and the last has progress report. It gives them a snapshot. It has the expectations.

Parent–teacher conferences turn into a short little conversation. This isn't the time to let you know your child is struggling. You already know and we are working on it.

Reimagined School Events

Too often the agenda of the back-to-school night is determined by school leaders and teachers, filled with lots of information and few opportunities for interaction. Yet how much more inclusive could they be if they are reimagined as spaces in which teachers, families, and students share their work. White (2009) uses video and tape recordings of student work during the traditional back-to-school night so that families can get a glimpse of the inner workings of the classroom.

Reading instruction in particular has changed a great deal in the past twenty years. Additionally, many families have been educated in different countries, with different cultural educational practices. Robin Moy, a third grade teacher in an urban school, uses videos to help families of primarily Chinese and Southeast Asian descent understand her reading instruction. She says, "I was telling parents I expected their kids to talk more but realized that didn't really mesh with their idea that kids should listen to the teacher." Robin asked a colleague to videotape several of her read-aloud sessions, including the turn-and-talk elements, and discussions so that she could share with families what she meant.

Jason Roberts in his fourth grade classroom asked his students to collaborate with him on what they thought their families should know and see of their reading workshop. They wanted their families to understand the Post-its they were using to keep track of their thinking, how they could sit in any place they wanted during independent reading time (as long as they were focused!), and to know more about their discussions. With Jason's help, they decided to interview each other about their class and videotape a discussion. Not only did it help the families see and hear what was happening in school, it demonstrated to families their children's great engagement and growing independence.

A report compiled by WestED (Zimmerman, 2017) documents teachers and school leaders using back-to-school nights in novel ways to engage parents academically with their children and in groups. Teachers share with parents some of the strategies in use in class, such as poetry reading and writing. Another idea is to try a "BIG WonderWall" on parents' night (Daniels, 2017, p. 47). Teachers create a large mural-like display with the words "I wonder …" on it. As parents arrive, they are invited to list questions and then browse, chat, and compare with other families.

Creating a physically open space that is accessible and inviting to families is also critical. A program called School In emphasizes positive interactions with reading and with books and the development of literacy nights. Program leaders created a space in the school with shelves of free books for children and adults. The teachers also created a project called Open Books—Open Minds. During this evening, they build mini-bookshelves, invite kids and families to paint them, and then have kids and parents come back to get books. This program used funds from Title I funding. "For us, because we work with these struggling readers, it's in the forefront. … We're always looking for ways to make reading fun. Sometimes, that gets lost," said one teacher.

Storytelling Evenings

Schools can provide structured support for teachers and families to bridge home, school, and community by holding storytelling evenings to share the pleasure in telling and listening to stories (see chapter 6 for further discussion). These events can help families engage by retelling a story, such as taking a familiar fairy or folktale and retelling, as a way to break the ice. Families and teachers can then begin telling more personal stories. Deceptively simple topics, such as talking about a birthday celebration or the story of my name, can provide powerful catalysts to family stories.

Using Technology to Create Literacy Bridges

Helping families have a window into their children's classroom through video is a great way to build a literacy bridge. Since teaching methods, classroom layouts, and even furniture and tools (think smart boards versus blackboards!) have changed, directing families to curated videos can go a long way in helping them understand what is going on in a classroom. A teacher can show families a video of a read-aloud session or shared reading to help parents understand how she is building concepts through careful attention to questions. These videos can be shown in conferences or can be uploaded to password-protected sites such as Vimeo or YouTube.

Students love creating videos of themselves. An application such as Flipgrid (flipgrid.com) supports brief videos of groups sharing an idea, experience, or other prompt. This provides students with a platform for their own ideas and an avenue for families to become part of the classroom community. Using video provides access to all students, and in particular supports struggling readers.

Want to Know More?

- Read *The Essential Conversation* by Sara Lawrence-Lightfoot (2003) for vivid stories about the complexity of teacher–parent relationships.
- Download a free app like Remind (www.remind.com) to communicate with families prior to report cards and parent–teacher conferences.
- Consider ways technology can expand parent–teacher conferences, with ideas from Fruin's (2016) blog post "6 Ways Technology Can Reinvent Parent-Teacher Conferences."

SUMMARY

To build authentic, productive relationships, it is critical to utilize multiple communication strategies. Elicit respect, and use families' questions and concerns about their children's literacy development in planning family engagement events. Remember to keep the student at the center of all discussions and work as a team to support him or her.

APPENDIX 3.1

Communicating with Families: A Self-Assessment

I communicate with parents through...

Individual phone calls or emails concerning student progress and general well-being

| Daily | Weekly | Monthly | Once a Marking Period | Once a School Year |

Paper or digital progress reports concerning academic progress and classroom behavior

| Daily | Weekly | Monthly | Once a Marking Period | Once a School Year |

Classwide email updates featuring due dates, homework tips, permission slip reminders, etc.

| Daily | Weekly | Monthly | Once a Marking Period | Once a School Year |

A classroom blog or webpage featuring current unit(s) of study, projects, school programs, field trips, etc.

| Daily | Weekly | Monthly | Once a Marking Period | Once a School Year |

Technological applications that provide notification of important updates, dates, or requests, such as Remind101, etc.

| Daily | Weekly | Monthly | Once a Marking Period | Once a School Year |

A monthly newsletter featuring student work samples, student comments, students' home connections to school programs and/or curricula

| Daily | Weekly | Monthly | Once a Marking Period | Once a School Year |

In-school celebrations, such as publishing parties, bulletin board unveilings, or project sharing

| Daily | Weekly | Monthly | Once a Marking Period | Once a School Year |

Recommendations for educational games, enrichment and/or supporting resources, homework help, and/or strategies for family involvement in curricula

| Daily | Weekly | Monthly | Once a Marking Period | Once a School Year |

Surveys of parents' comments, questions, and suggestions for connecting upcoming curricula (projects, text selection, etc.) to home cultures, interests, and lifestyles

| Daily | Weekly | Monthly | Once a Marking Period | Once a School Year |

Parents communicate with me through...

Individual phone calls or emails concerning student progress and general well-being

| Daily | Weekly | Monthly | Once a Marking Period | Once a School Year |

Comments and/or questions on paper or digital progress reports concerning academic progress and classroom behavior

| Daily | Weekly | Monthly | Once a Marking Period | Once a School Year |

Replies to classwide email updates with relevant at-home updates

| Daily | Weekly | Monthly | Once a Marking Period | Once a School Year |

Comments and/or photo replies on the classroom blog or webpage

| Daily | Weekly | Monthly | Once a Marking Period | Once a School Year |

Replies to technological applications concerning important updates, dates, or requests, such as Remind101, etc.

| Daily | Weekly | Monthly | Once a Marking Period | Once a School Year |

Submissions for the monthly newsletter, such as photos, interviews, comments, or surveys that connect to school programs and/or curricula

| Daily | Weekly | Monthly | Once a Marking Period | Once a School Year |

Attendance at in-school celebrations, such as publishing parties, bulletin board unveilings, or project sharing

| Daily | Weekly | Monthly | Once a Marking Period | Once a School Year |

Assistance in the development of in-school celebrations, such as agenda-setting, fundraising, materials management, etc.

| Daily | Weekly | Monthly | Once a Marking Period | Once a School Year |

Updates concerning the utility and/or efficacy of teacher-recommended games, resources, or homework tips

Daily	Weekly	Monthly	Once a Marking Period	Once a School Year

Comments, questions, and suggestions for connecting upcoming curricula (projects, text selection, etc.) to home cultures, interests, and lifestyles

Daily	Weekly	Monthly	Once a Marking Period	Once a School Year

Chapter 4

Generating Respect for Home and Community Literacy Experiences

---

GUIDING PRINCIPLE THREE

Teachers can build bridges of understanding between home and school by respecting and honoring families' out-of-school literacy experiences as springboards for literacy explorations.

Natalee Vilcek accepted an invitation to return to her elementary alma mater in order to get to know her daughter's kindergarten teacher through the school's Jump Start program. This three-week summer-school program provided five year olds, family members, and teachers an occasion to start building relationships while exploring academic and social expectations. During weekly parent sessions, Natalee heard about upcoming monthly family literacy gatherings for parents, held throughout the school year. As a stay-at-home mom, Natalee's flexible schedule allowed her to attend two of four family gatherings.

During the second gathering in January, she learned of the Family Literacy Photo Project, an out-of-school learning engagement designed to help teachers explore visual evidence of families' rich everyday reading interactions (Street, 2001). She eagerly joined in this project with help from her daughter Kristina, her husband, and three older girls. During one week in February, they captured photos of Kristina and family members exploring everyday texts such as menus or school supplies at the drugstore in the midst of their community and home lives (see figure 4.1).

Kristina reading at drug store	Kisha reading at home

Figure 4.1. Family Photos

Marian White, who grew up in a nearby urban center, could not accept the invitation due to her work in the food-service industry. In September, she received another invitation to join kindergarten parents at bimonthly family literacy gatherings held in the morning before school. As a single mother of two, these events still did not fit into her work or family commitments.

Mindful of parents' work and family obligations, kindergarten teachers Vicki and Lisa collaborated with their student teachers, Abby and Ariana, to design a family photo project to send home to ensure that all families had access to the project. Halfway through the year, Marian received a third invitation explaining the Family Literacy Photo Project.

Kindergarten families were invited to take photos of their children reading "anytime, anywhere" (Lopez & Caspe, 2014) outside of school, reading anything *other* than a book. She enthusiastically participated with her kindergarten daughter, Kisha, and younger daughter. Like Natalee, she spent a week in February taking numerous photos of her children interacting with texts such as grocery ads and iPhones in personal, productive ways (figure 4.1). Both mothers helped create a literacy "lifeline" between families and teachers.

These family literacy pictures did not portray Kisha or Kristina as students who struggled with reading. Natalee and Marian learned their kindergarten girls were identified as below-average readers, according to a state-mandated literacy assessment, during their parent–teacher conferences in October. Thirty-five percent of students in this high-needs suburban school were identified as struggling readers that year. In contrast to this school literacy label, both families returned photographic evidence of their daughters as motivated readers outside of school.

Like other parent and grandparent participants in this photo project at Clairton Elementary, Natalee and Marian were not shy about explaining why they loved their town. The lack of segregation distinguished this suburb from nearby urban, rural, and suburban cities in the northeastern United States. The constant mingling of people from different ethnic backgrounds (Greek, Puerto Rican, African American, Slovak, and Italian) was an asset parents eagerly shared. In spite of significant disparity across household incomes (a quarter of families lived below poverty level while a quarter were labeled as middle or upper income), parents frequently shared unsolicited, prideful comments about their community life. This former steel mill town appeared intent on rebounding, seen in wide-ranging community celebrations, religious activities and school sports, music and theater events, bringing diverse families together.

Parents and grandparents provided visual evidence of kindergarten readers with family members making use of everyday, out-of-school texts in functional ways to entertain themselves, consider household purchases, explore community life, and more (Duke & Purcell-Gates, 2003; Goodman, Watson, & Burke, 1996; Janks, 2014; Rowsell, 2006). Photos portrayed thriving, not struggling, readers outside of school. Kress (2005) reminds teachers of the need to uncover and respect the vast array of literacy interactions in children's lives beyond school in this way. "Unless we understand the principles of meaning making in all the ways in which children do, we won't … really understand the ways in which they try to make sense of print" (p. xvi).

Our third family–school literacy principle stems from our need to build a literacy bridge or photographic "lifeline," bringing together two previously disconnected literacy worlds. Teachers can use family literacy photos to obtain a new appreciation and respect for the multiple literacies in homes and communities (Street, 1995) in hopes of obtaining a broader lens on readers. We recognize: *Teachers can build bridges of understanding between home and school by respecting and honoring families' out-of-school literacy experiences as springboards for literacy explorations.*

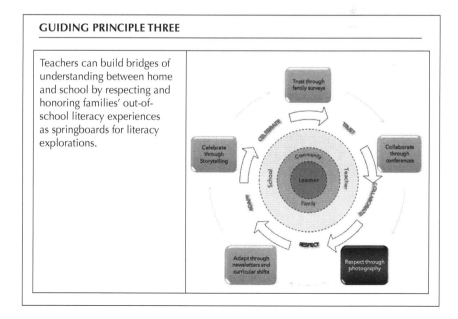

GUIDING PRINCIPLE THREE

Teachers can build bridges of understanding between home and school by respecting and honoring families' out-of-school literacy experiences as springboards for literacy explorations.

INSIGHTS FROM RESEARCH INTO A
SOCIOCULTURAL VIEW OF LITERACY

Sociocultural Perspective on Family Literacy

As mothers, Natalee and Marian returned to school likely carrying a conventional mindset regarding teachers' expectations of families and reading events at home (see chapter 2 for further discussion). In the 1980s and 1990s, when Natalee and Marian attended elementary school, it was common for teachers to hold a deficit perspective on home literacy experiences within high-needs families (Caspe, 2003; Dudley-Marling & Lucas, 2009). Finders and Lewis (1994) explain the ramifications of this limited view:

> The institutional view of nonparticipating parents remains based on a deficit model. "Those who need to come, don't come," a teacher explains, revealing an assumption that one of the main reasons for involving parents is to remediate them. It is assumed that involved parents bring a body of knowledge about the purposes of schooling to match institutional knowledge. Unless they bring such knowledge to the school, they themselves are thought to need education in becoming legitimate participants. (p. 50)

At that time, many educators struggled to consider the usefulness of valuing and building upon children's multiple literacies acquired outside of the classroom, especially those of struggling readers (Street, 1995). The dominant use of commercial reading programs consisting of basalized children's literature with controlled vocabulary was evident in most U.S. elementary classrooms (Goodman, Shannon, Freeman, & Murphy, 1988), devoid of everyday texts children encounter outside of school. We wonder if many parents of struggling readers like Natalee and Marian recognize this devaluing lens and therefore do not accept teachers' invitations to become learning partners.

In contrast to this deficit model, the 1980s became a generative era for a small group of literacy researchers investigating out-of-school literacies, seen as a sociocultural perspective on family literacy (Auerbach, 1989; Dudley-Marling, 2009). Emilia Ferreiro and Ana Teberosky (1982) in Argentina; Gordon Wells (1980) in England; Shirley Brice Heath (1983) in Appalachia; and Denny Taylor and Catherine Dorsey-Gaines (1988) in New York each offer an alternative view of teaching reading "responsive to the literacy worlds of marginalized children" (Purcell-Gates, 2006, p. 166).

Ferreiro and Teberosky (1982) urge classroom teachers to intentionally think about building on the rich literacy foundation children unconsciously acquire at home and in their community before school in this way: "It is absurd to imagine that four and five-year-old children growing up in urban environments that display print everywhere (on toys, on billboards and road

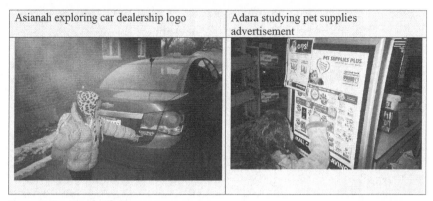

Figure 4.2. Family Photos

signs, on their clothes, on TV) do not develop any ideas about this cultural object until they find themselves sitting before a teacher" (p. 12) (see figure 4.2). They advise teachers to stop limiting their vision of the literacy strengths each child brings to school. Johnson-Parsons (2010) reiterates the importance of differences, diverse learning styles, backgrounds, cultures, and other unique characteristics of children, easily ignored if teachers hold onto the deficit model or narrow assessment lens.

This appeal to respect families' literacy foundation or literate identity is important to all learners, in particular families with struggling readers (Aukerman, 2015; White, 2009). Readers who struggle with text frequently experience a significant disconnect between everyday texts found in their homes and school literacy texts such as basals with controlled vocabulary and worksheets presenting skills and words in isolation (Duke & Purcell-Gates, 2003; McTavish, 2007). Assessment tools like the Family Literacy Photo Project are chosen to identify the strengths as well as struggles students bring to literacy events in and out of school.

The joint National Council of Teachers of English and International Literacy Association Standards for Assessment of Reading and Writing (NCTE/ILA, 2009) urge teachers to see assessment as a process of inquiry by

1. Gathering and using "multiple perspectives" on each reader,
2. Considering the "socially complex nature of reading and writing and the important roles of school and home" in literacy development, and
3. Involving families as "active, essential participants in the assessment process."

Literacy strengths and struggles shared by family members become important factors for teachers to explore, especially when they are not aware of students' diverse cultural and social literacy foundation.

Ada (2003) reminds us how "students live in two worlds: home and school. If these two worlds do not recognize, understand and respect each other, students are put into a difficult predicament" and learning becomes a struggle (p. 11). Uncovering and utilizing out-of-school texts for instruction (in addition to mandated school district texts) needs to become teachers' focus, as they set out to respect and build on children's foundational literacy world from their homes and communities.

Everyday Texts to Expand Literate Identities

The terms *everyday texts* or *out-of-school literacies* evolve from a socio-cultural lens on literacy. Paulo Freire's transformative inquiry (1987) involving Brazilian "illiterate" peasants provides teachers with a broader view of reading instruction by offering paradigm-shifting demonstrations of how readers simultaneously read their world (environment) while reading words. "Because readers are agentive constructors of meaning with their own personal and cultural frames of reference, texts never have a sole single meaning for all readers; what counts as good reading is determined culturally and changes over time" (Aukerman, 2015, p. 57).

For example, when struggling readers like Kisha or Kristina explore a grocery store advertisement sent to their home, they use their own socially and culturally acquired knowledge, mental images of stores filled with food items, information about the foods family members enjoy, or visual images of food to help them understand the printed words on the ad. Reading is seen as a unique cultural and social interaction with print for each learner.

When teachers perceive literacy as both social and cultural experiences, reading instruction evolves into a more significant event beyond decoding to pronounce words accurately for assessment records. Research within "new literacy studies" led by Brian Street (1995), emphasizing the use of everyday texts in school, inspires teachers to search further than the typical texts used with struggling readers, such as basals, high-interest and low-vocabulary anthologies, and decodable readers, toward multiple literacies evident in home and community lives.

Voss's (1996) exploration demonstrates how four struggling readers and their families reveal their most "powerful literacies that remain unknown and uncelebrated in school" (p. 201). Tapping into students' diverse literacies for instructional purposes provides new avenues for reading success and broadens teachers' understanding of meaning making beyond school events.

Goodman, Watson, and Burke (1996) examine everyday texts by outlining four functions of literacy in students' lives, accentuating the social and cultural nature of reading. They identify common forms of reading such as contact lists of phone numbers on an iPhone, Sunday comics, stock reports,

Figure 4.3. Functions of Literacy in Homes and Communities

Goodman, Watson, and Burke (1996) *Four Functions of Literacy*	Johnson (2010) *Seven Functions of Literacy*
Environmental To survive in the world	*Instrumental* To manage everyday life
Recreational For pleasure	*Recreational* For pleasure and enjoyment *Interactional* To maintain relationships *Spiritual* For religious purposes
Occupational Job related	*Educational* To increase knowledge
Informational To gain information	*Instrumental* To manage everyday life (repeat) *News Related* To gain information about local to international events *Financial* To apply for loans, manage budgets, and more

and fast food nutritional facts, sorting these into four general categories of reading: environmental, recreational, occupational, and informational. They invite teachers to build on "the literacy learning that already takes place in the home" in order to broaden the forms of literacy used for classroom instruction (p. 21). Johnson (2010) identifies seven similar purposes for reading within an African American intergenerational family (see figure 4.3).

Collectively, Johnson (2010) and Goodman, Watson, and Burke (1996) nudge teachers to wonder why these literacy encounters are so undervalued for instructional purposes at school. These everyday or comfortable texts, print readily available in children's homes and communities, provide an inviting bridge into the world of school texts for children and their families.

In an effort to bridge home and school literacies, Duke and Purcell-Gates (2003) encourage teachers to connect new forms of literacy readers encounter at school with familiar forms from homes and communities. In their exploration alongside hundreds of low-income, emergent readers from the Boston area, they identify genres or forms of literacy common in homes and schools, like recipes, money, price tags, and ads. They urge teachers to find avenues for building on children's literacy strengths acquired from home for phonics, writing, and reading work during classroom instruction.

Out-of-school literacies offer significant potential to expand all readers' (but especially struggling readers') literate identity. "Culture, personal experience, interest, and context are all likely to influence a child's repertoire of practices and thus shape the child's literate identity" (Aukerman, 2015, p. 57).

Creating opportunities for families and children to inform teachers about their out-of-school literate lives helps to expand readers' self-perceptions. Teachers need encouragement to examine everyday texts in order to broaden their definition of literacy and rethink labels like "struggling reader." When educators acknowledge family members' essential role as vital literacy partners, they send a message conveying their respect for each family's unique ability to support their child's growth.

Curricular Potentials Revealed through Photographs

Common Core State Standards (CCSS), coupled with new teacher evaluation systems tying teacher assessment to their students' end-of-year test scores, tend to limit educators' use of diverse texts, especially out-of-school literacies. Reading and language CCSS emphasize the use of children's books containing complex text. An analysis of the kindergarten and first grade storybooks suggested by CCSS revealed multiple dilemmas with these supposed text exemplars, such as the use of older books published before 1978, a lack of multicultural books, and texts featuring animals not people (Short, 2013). Such a limited vision of children's literature for classroom instruction, devoid of rich contemporary books, can readily lead readers to conclude that texts used at school are not relevant to their lives (Short, 2013, p. 3). Within our Common Core era, it is no wonder that teachers struggle to consider the use of out-of-school literacies for classroom instruction.

Nonetheless, educators who value a sociocultural perspective on family literacy continue to create literacy bridges, letting families know they respect and want to build on their multiple literacies acquired outside of school. The power of photography to capture significant literacy moments in and out of school proves to be an overlooked yet powerful avenue for learning with families. Whitmore's preschool drama inquiry (2015) demonstrates the purposeful nature of photos to reveal far more than field notes by removing verbal language. Her unintentional use of photographs to explore drama as a way of knowing for preschoolers became her "most productive means of data collection" (p. 28) for this project, allowing teachers to visually dissect children's learning moments.

In New York City, Spielman (2001) introduces her collaborative yearlong photo project to low-income Latino families in this way: "Schools need to hear what learning goes on in your homes so that teachers can build on that learning. We will use cameras so you can show all the ways that your culture,

Petros and dad enjoying Sunday comics	Gauge and grandma exploring fast food nutrition facts

Figure 4.4

your family, and your community are teachers for your children" (p. 764). Upon gathering photos, teachers and families study visual artifacts/photos of parents teaching about literacy, technology, science, culture, and more. (See Figure 4.4 for similar photos from Clairton families.) To complete the project, families share their learning photos with teachers and graduate students who use newfound insights as resources to inform their instructional decisions and interactions with learners.

In an effort to move beyond a limited perspective of family literacy seen in the familiar practice of mothers reading storybooks to children, Mui and Anderson (2008) spent time learning from an Indo-American family of fifteen children and adults in British Columbia. Over several months, they observed family members engaging with a plethora of texts, slowly understanding how the Johar home presents "a rich tapestry of language and literacy practices" (p. 236).

Instead of finding storybook reading at home, they discover a wealth of social and cultural literacy events like board games; Punjabi, Tagalog, and English conversations; Punjabi and English songs; along with traditional skill and drill workbooks and school math projects. The researchers conclude by emphasizing the learning potential of literacy diaries, photo literacy projects, or literacy artifacts that can broaden teachers' appreciation for each reader's strengths, gained through collaborative, everyday interactions with their out-of-school literacy partners.

Matson's (2013) inquiry with struggling high school readers in a required reading class reveals her ability to create a trustworthy classroom space where students develop their own literacy histories using multimedia tools. Adolescents offer her a rare window on their lives outside of school as they capture photos and audio recordings and take notes to gather evidence of how their out-of-school literacy experiences connect to in-school literacy events.

Matson's intent to provide "opportunities to use their own literacy strengths" (2013, p. 15) proves noteworthy as struggling readers reveal a breadth and depth of everyday literacy events, including one teenager's project showing reading events encountered by his two-year-old child. Another student's literacy interactions display evidence of reading and writing encounters during construction work with his father. Matson's multimodal understanding of her students' literate lives outside of school drives her to continue weaving their social and cultural literacy knowledge into subsequent curricular engagements.

Across these complex literacy explorations, teachers working with struggling readers are invited to think about how families' out-of-school literacies can be used to "transform the educational process in order to align it more closely" with students' distinct cultural and social knowledge" (King, 1994; p. 27). These inquiries using authentic, everyday texts look quite different from typical programs for struggling readers touted by What Works Clearinghouse (n.d.).

Decontextualized texts in Read Naturally, Wilson Reading System, Success for All, and Open Court Reading rarely inspire or motivate reluctant readers. Research studies built around texts with controlled vocabulary continue to limit teachers' vision of the learning potential in homes and communities and the possibilities within everyday texts, hidden quietly away in children's homes until teachers ask students and families to share.

Redefining literacy according to families and communities, not just schools (Hull and Schultz, 2002; Purcell-Gates, 2006), takes courageous teachers like Vicki, Lisa, Abby, and Ariana, willing to look beyond the text exemplars and commercial reading programs offered in most school districts. They set out to overcome reading curricula that leave "no space for the real-life literacies of students" (White, 2009, p. 438). Harnessing the potential of photography to record fertile literacy moments away from school in order to respect and use families' out-of-school texts for literacy engagements at school requires a broader teacher vision of literacy learning.

3, 2, 1 STOP AND THINK

3. **Identify three** out-of-school reading experiences your students and families value.
2. **Think about two** ways you can show parents your respect for their family's literate lives beyond school, specifically their everyday literacy interactions with their children.
1. **Consider one** way you can use photography to capture hidden literacy moments at school, images that help families reimagine and value their vital role as literacy partners outside of school.

DEVELOPING RESPECT THROUGH
FAMILY ENGAGEMENTS

Natalee Vilcek and Marian White, the two kindergarten moms whose stories open this chapter, offered teachers photographic evidence of their children naturally participating in authentic, socially meaningful literacy events outside school (Purcell-Gates & Duke, 2004). Their children's teachers, Vicki and Lisa, with student teachers Abby and Ariana, set out to examine family photos in order to investigate the dichotomy between two separate reading worlds, making some children appear to be "non-reader[s] in school while using print for significant purposes in life [outside school]" (Taylor, 1982, p. 548).

Teachers chose "to bridge the gap between home and school so that reading in one [was seen as] reading in the other" (Taylor, 1982, p. 548). Family photos were solicited in order to build literacy bridges, uniting home and school reading interactions in an effort "to connect people and places" (Latham, 2012).

What follows is an overview of three components comprising our Family Literacy Photo Project:

• Collection of family photos by students and families
• Categorization, analysis, and making sense of photos
• Creation of classroom literacy engagements using photos along with other authentic out-of-school texts

Within each component, we present the specific steps to enact this project. With each step, we share how teachers engage in learning more about the literacy practices of their students and their families. And because families are invited to be collaborators in this work, they get a unique, real-life lens on their child's literacy strengths evolving from out-of-school experiences.

To get an overall understanding of the intention and scope of the project, we present a graphic organizer of the three components and the action steps within each component in figure 4.5. In the sections that follow, more detail and examples of each step are provided.

COMPONENT 1: COLLECTING EVERYDAY
FAMILY LITERACY PHOTOS

Teachers can modify the following steps or develop their own steps to gather family photos, according to their literacy goals, the availability of cameras, and the level of engagement with families.

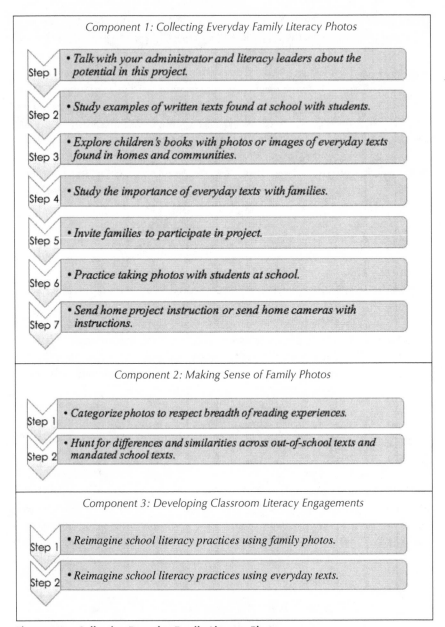

Figure 4.5.   Collecting Everyday Family Literacy Photos

Step 1: Talk with your administrator and literacy leaders about the potential of a Family Literacy Photo Project.

Title I funding and special education regulations require administrators, literacy leaders, and teachers to provide annual family–school interactions.

Administrators need support to build productive learning bridges with students' families throughout the year. Sharing professional development readings like Spielman's (2001) study or Endrizzi's (2016) inquiry offers school leaders a vision of the potential in a photo project.

Discussing confidentiality issues up front with your administrators before gathering family photos helps avoid complications later on. Today teenagers and adults alike offer a barrage of visual images revealing their private lives through social media (e.g., Facebook, Snapchat, and Instagram). Mindful of this accessibility to private lives, most school districts send out general photo permission consent forms to all families. Some administrators might want to avoid photo-sharing sites. Inexpensive disposable cameras can be purchased instead.

Step 2: Study examples of written texts found at school with students.

In order to expand readers' literate identities as well as teachers' literacy vision, classroom conversations about reading as an anytime, anywhere event (Lopez & Caspe, 2014) are highly useful. We started by initiating a hunt for texts at school (see figures 4.6 and 4.7). Capturing environmental literacy walks throughout the school building using an iPhone allows for extended conversations. Teachers across grade levels can ask students to record examples of everyday texts in journals.

Displaying these literacy photos on the smart board allows teachers to launch conversations with students about the value of reading at school and

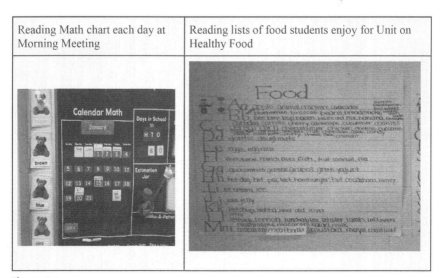

Reading Math chart each day at Morning Meeting	Reading lists of food students enjoy for Unit on Healthy Food

Figure 4.6.

Figure 4.7. Preschool class story about a lost license plate

beyond. Considering questions like who is reading and why they are reading helps students begin to consider a larger need for reading, beyond their instruction at school. For a lesson plan and resources, see http://readwritethink.org/classroom-resources/lesson-plans/from-stop-signs-golden-27.html.

Step 3: Explore children's books with photos or images of everyday texts found in homes and communities.

Children's books with photos or illustrations depicting print in home and community lives become useful at this stage. Teachers can share children's books like *I Read Signs* (Hoban, 1987), *Last Stop on Market Street* (de la Peña, 2015), and *The 13th Clue* (Jonas, 1992), emphasizing written texts found throughout communities and in homes, during classroom read-aloud experiences. (See appendix 4.1 for a list of other books for use across grade levels.) Class conversations driven by questions like "Who/what/why are children and adults reading?" help to enlarge children's literate identities beyond school reading engagements.

Teachers across grade levels might extend this notion of reading occurring outside of school by asking students to keep a reading log of what/where/with whom they read for several days. Families can be invited to join this exploration through a family newsletter that outlines the value of reading anytime and anywhere (see also chapter 5 on family newsletters).

Step 4: Study the importance of everyday texts with students' families.

Teachers need time for literacy conversations with families. Demonstrating respect for family members as each student's first literacy role model can occur across various venues, including family newsletters using Remind. me, parent conferences, and family literacy gatherings. We initiated parent–teacher conversations during family gatherings to investigate the power of everyday texts. Each family received a free copy of *I Read Signs* (Hoban, 1987), used to launch discussions about when, where, and why we read in our lives. We emphasized family members' overlooked role as essential literacy partners, thanking them for their quiet, vital support. Teachers might also want to create a PowerPoint slide show of community street signs, campaign signs, store signs, even signs on food items from grocery stores to extend this conversation. Children's books coupled with a PowerPoint slide show can spark "Aha!" moments as parents recognize their vital role.

Family newsletters can become a substitute for family gatherings. Highlighting books with everyday texts and community photos depicting community signage allows families with busy schedules and work commitments to participate (see figure 4.8).

Step 5: Invite families to participate in the Family Literacy Photo Project.

Open-ended invitations with simple instructions welcome families to participate and become key learning partners with teachers (see figure 4.9).

Step 6: Practice taking photos with students.

Capturing meaningful photos starts by helping children explore what constitutes a "thoughtful or important" photo. Showing children how to take photos using an iPhone camera is an easy place to start. Our photo project involving disposable cameras required us to establish simple, clear directions for kindergarten photographers but was easy and relatively low cost.

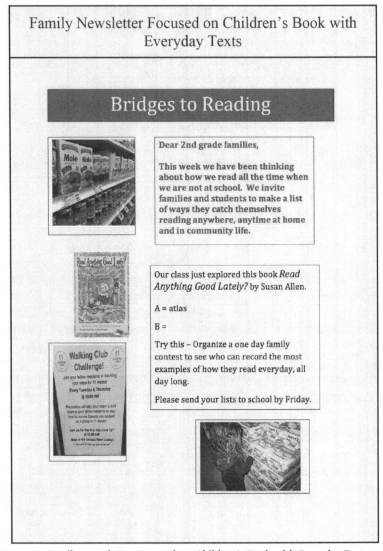

Family Newsletter Focused on Children's Book with Everyday Texts

Bridges to Reading

Dear 2nd grade families,

This week we have been thinking about how we read all the time when we are not at school. We invite families and students to make a list of ways they catch themselves reading anywhere, anytime at home and in community life.

Our class just explored this book *Read Anything Good Lately?* by Susan Allen.

A = atlas

B =

Try this – Organize a one day family contest to see who can record the most examples of how they read everyday, all day long.

Please send your lists to school by Friday.

Figure 4.8.   Family Newsletter Focused on Children's Book with Everyday Texts

Creating brief practice photo sessions at school with small student groups using disposable or digital cameras enables all children to become more seasoned photographers. Sharing digital photos through the classroom smart board the same day helps younger children learn techniques for capturing images that show others (or do not show others) how students and families read everywhere.

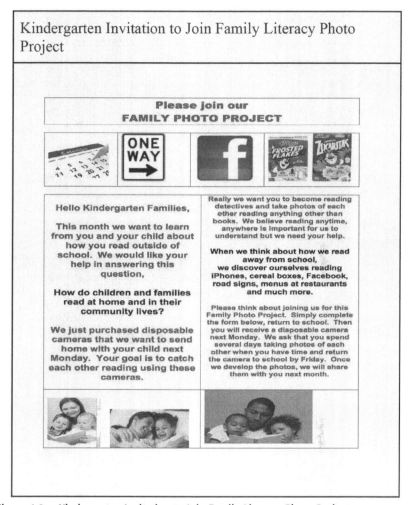

Figure 4.9.   Kindergarten Invitation to Join Family Literacy Photo Project

Step 7: Send home cameras with instructions.

If teachers receive permission to gather photos using social media like Snapchat or via their school email, they can share instructions via the classroom web page or Remind.me (see figure 4.10). At this time, teachers might choose to send home photo consent forms as well, giving permission to share photos with other families in coming weeks.

Fruitful family–school collaborations evolve from thoughtful planning and preparation by teachers. We spent two weeks preparing kindergarten photographers and families to join our photo project.

Family Instructions for Photo Project

---

1. **Look:** Watch everywhere you go to see if you can "catch" someone reading anything besides books! They could be reading signs, cereal boxes, or recipes.
2. **Stop:** Stop what you are doing and stand still so you can take your picture.
3. **Wind:** Wind the back of the camera each time before you take a picture.
4. **Point:** Point the camera in the direction of the picture you want to take.
5. **Click:** Press the oval button on top of the camera to take your pictures!

Figure 4.10. Family Instructions for Photo Project

COMPONENT 2: MAKING SENSE OF FAMILY PHOTOS

Teachers can adapt the following steps or develop their own analysis to unpack family photos in light of their literacy goals. Rowe and Fain's (2013) family bilingual book project, emphasizing the need to "respect and encourage home literacy practices" (p. 403) rather than tell families what they need to do, maintains a focus on learning from families. Spending time reviewing and considering the meanings within the photos honors families.

Step 1: Categorize photos to respect breadth and depth of reading experiences outside of school.

Goodman, Watson, and Burke (1996) and Johnson (2010) offer educators a broad view of the potential in everyday texts at school and home (see figure 4.3). Environmental texts like road signs help us survive in the world, recreational texts like computer games offer pleasure reading moments, occupational texts support job-related tasks, while informational texts like maps help us obtain useful information. These four functions can help teachers look for different types of reading interactions depicted within family photos.

In figure 4.11 you can see how student teachers Abby and Ariana used Goodman, Watson, and Burke's (1996) categories to sort the photographs they received from their students and their families, and figure 4.12 is an example of the photographs and their categories.

Our analysis centered on the question "What is the photographer telling us about literacy?" Family photos show literacy woven into "the fabric of family life" (Taylor, 1982, p. 549). We noted images portraying motivated and engaged readers, not struggling learners. Our respect for families as literacy partners increased as we noted "rich and extensive legacies of literacy" (Johnson, 2010, p. 41) accumulating over time outside of school. We wondered how to build on this rich legacy during school literacy engagements.

When teachers send home cameras asking for parental input, literacy learning becomes a shared responsibility between home and school. Family

Purposeful Literacy in Home and Community Lives

Functions of Literacy

*(Everyday Reading and Writing Experiences
Woven into the Fabric of Our Lives)*

K. Goodman Functions, 1996	Kindergarten families' examples
Environmental *To survive in world* 38 photos	Weekly advertisement (5), cereal box (4), food label (4), recipes (3), store name (2) , store bag (2), TV Stand box (1), DVD box (1), gift card sign (1), cookie cake (1), Mall sign (1), fast food ad (1), stop sign (1), Handicap sign (1), sale sign (1), price tag (1), coloring book (1), shampoo (1),restaurant name (1), salt/pepper shakers (1), chlorox bottle (1), water bottle (1), car name (1), wet floor sign (1)
Recreational *For pleasure* 28 photos	Texting (3), magazines (3), iPad (3), picture book (3), book (3), board game (2), newspaper (2), alphabet & numbers (1), computer (1), DVD case (1), CD (1), Valentine's box (1), activity/game book (1), flash cards (1), Santa letter (1), puzzle (1)
Occupational *Job related* 4 photos	Lesson plan (1), keyboard (1), homework (1), text book (1)
Informational *To gain information* 23 photos	Menu (4), Mall rules/directions (2), newspaper flyer (2),Mall pamphlet (1), store hours sign (1), TV guide book (1), dictionary (1), thermostat (1), medicine label (1), TV listing (1), planner (1), solar system placemat (1), Valentine's list (1), Disney pamphlet (1), car dealership (1), calendar (1), newspaper (1), first aid directions (1)

Figure 4.11.   Abby and Ariana's Family Photos according to Functions of Literacy

Recreational Reading = iPad interactions to relax at the end of day	Informational Reading = solar system placement interactions to gather new ideas

Figure 4.12

members and children become teachers' literacy informants (Harste, 1986). As photographers, they portray their literacy knowledge visually, proving to teachers how literacy engagements occur quietly but thoughtfully throughout family life. We believe families gain a newfound respect for teachers when they realize their input is a valuable resource for learning.

Step 2: Hunt for differences and similarities across out-of-school texts and mandated school texts.

Making sense of family photos occurs over time. Taking time to digest the wealth of out-of-school reading interactions allows teachers to think broadly about implications for classroom practice. Duke and Purcell-Gates's (2003) comparison of text genres from home and school helps to identify unique forms of purposeful reading interactions from home lives for exploration at school. Some of the genres they found in both school and home include labels, signs, messages, calendars, schedules, songs, children's and adult books, and newspapers.

Unlike data collection tools such as observational notes, photos quietly capture visual information such as emotions and relationships (Whitmore, 2015). Photos taken by family members place them in a leadership role as informants. We witnessed young and older readers enjoying, laughing, and making decisions based on personal interests. Motivation and engagement with purposeful texts was evident across literacy interactions (Skilton-Sylvester, 2002).

Questions to guide our photo analysis included:

1. How do families read purposefully outside of school?
2. How do family members unknowingly or knowingly support their child's literacy growth in their daily lives?
3. What can teachers learn about family literacy practices in order to build connections between known literacies from home life to unknown school literacies?

Literate identities from home life contrasted sharply with school literate identities. Figure 4.13 helps teachers privilege out-of-school literacy interactions in an effort to understand children's familiar literate ways of knowing in order to adapt and revise school literacy practices.

Differences between out-of-school and in-school texts emphasized the meaningful nature of family literacy interactions. Making sense of information motivated readers and inspired confidence not always seen at school. A plethora of genres chosen by families was not uncommon, but these literacy funds of knowledge often disappeared at school. Teachers often

Figure 4.13. A Sampling of Kindergarten Home and School Literacy Experiences Across Sociocultural Contexts

Literacy context	What read?	Motivation and engagement to expand literate identity
HOME	Santa letter framed on wall Email on iPad Sunday newspaper comics Grocery shopping ads	High Readers chose whole, complex texts to enjoy, explore, and make shopping decisions
COMMUNITY	Menu at fast food restaurant Playground rules at mall play area Colored markers at drug store	High Readers chose texts to make food selections, remember rules, or make shopping decisions
SCHOOL *Small-group interactions*	Basal decodable texts—Can we? We can! . . .	Lower Readers struggle to see purpose in test-prep reading texts mandated by school curriculum
Small-group interactions— shared or guided reading	Leveled readers and authentic literature	Medium Readers experience varying levels of purpose using texts chosen by the teacher
Centers	iPads or computers— Starfall, i-Ready, etc.	Lower medium Readers might struggle to see purpose in reading test-prep computer programs purchased by the district
Whole-class interactions	Morning message on smart board—circle letters we know, circle words we know. . .	Medium Readers experience whole texts first and then explore phonics minilessons
Whole-class interactions for read-aloud sessions	Winter big books	High Readers explore complex texts to enjoy and discover ideas chosen by teachers
Individual explorations for independent reading	Leveled readers and authentic literature	Lower high Readers chose texts to enjoy and explore

narrowed reading opportunities by adhering to district-mandated curriculum. When reading events were reduced to memorization and phonics skills, a teacher focus due to mandated state reading assessments tied to their annual teaching evaluations, motivation and engagement seemed to diminish. We set out to make literacy interactions at school more meaningful and purposeful.

COMPONENT 3: DEVELOPING CLASSROOM LITERACY ENGAGEMENTS

Teachers can select, adapt, and gain inspiration using any of the following reading engagements.

Step 1: Reimagine school literacy practices using family photos.

A driving force in our literacy decisions focused on letting families know we respected and valued their substantial role as literacy learning partners. Voss's (1996) insights on valuing hidden literacies from home remained uppermost in our minds: "Our society asks that schools teach children to be literate, but values only certain literacies and remains uncertain of how to develop others" (p. 188). Families needed to hear teachers thank them for broadening their view of reading beyond school hours (see figure 4.14). Going public and responding to family literacy insights remained a constant focus.

Step 2: Reimagine school literacy practices using everyday texts.

An alternative to gathering family photos is collecting everyday texts through a home–school project. Family newsletters can launch the search by inviting family members to send to school everyday text samples they gather over a week. Everyday texts like cereal boxes, grocery ads, and menus can be used as manipulatives for an array of literacy interactions at school.

Kindergarten reading instruction dominated by national literacy standards continues to emphasize teaching phonics in isolation. Our family photos demonstrated a broader reading perspective shared by Hornsby and Wilson (2010), who offer detailed examples of how to teach phonics within meaningful reading contexts. We chose to develop literacy engagements with whole texts first, followed by reading skill and strategy minilessons using the same texts (see figure 4.15).

When teachers respect family members' essential role as vibrant literacy partners, their view of literacy learning is expanded far beyond classroom hours. They seek opportunities to build on authentic, meaningful literacy knowledge obtained in hidden, natural literacy interactions occurring daily in homes and communities. Literacy learning as a shared responsibility

Figure 4.14.   **Re-imagined School Literacy Practices Using Family Literacy Photos**

Literacy Instruction	Engagements to Explore at School	
	Kindergarten	1st–4th grade
We Read Anytime, Anywhere bulletin board	• Each student chooses one photo and writes about what and why like to read. • Strive to emphasize multiple home languages when possible. • For students whose families did not submit photos, take photos at school with child holding an everyday text of their choice.	Write a family story using family photo or create a family story.

I can read
HerShe.
at hom.
I like to read
with mi Gdmu

Literacy Centers	• Write about classmates' photos.	Write to classmates posing questions.
Morning Meeting or Read-Aloud Time	• Study family photos as a class; invite students to illustrate when they read with their families at home. • Read whole texts first, then continue to hunt for sight words hidden in photos, create lists, operation game—make, him, or, the . . . Comics—and, for, is, of . . .	Write letters to families thanking them for being important reading partners.
Read-Aloud Time	• Highlight a range of texts explored at home; share recipe books, maps, magazines, comics, CD cases.	Same.

Figure 4.14 *(Cont.)*

Literacy Instruction	Engagements to Send Home to Families	
	Kindergarten	1st–4th grade
Literacy Photo Book	• Each child chooses one photo; create class photo book to send home to families. • For children who did not send photos, gather everyday text examples and take their photo to use for book.	Create literacy autobiographies using photos gathered over time.

Monthly Family Newsletters	• Insert several photos each month to thank families for their continued support as reading partners.	Same.

encompasses children's diverse literate worlds, both at home and in school. Teachers open a world of literate possibilities by respecting the unique, rich learning spaces outside of school.

SUMMARY

To develop respect for family members' roles as first literacy partners, gather evidence of rich literate lives away from school through family literacy photos. Ask families to send to school literacy photos or everyday texts in order to

Figure 4.15.   Re-imagined School Literacy Practices Using Families' Everyday Texts

Literacy Activity	Engagements to Explore at School	
	Kindergarten	1st–4th grade
Classroom alphabet on wall	• Redesign alphabet on classroom wall using A–Z examples of everyday text. • Strive to share multiple languages. • Extend classroom alphabet by brainstorming *G* words we know using families' funds of knowledge.	Expand vocabulary by inviting students to select words of importance from everyday text.
Morning Meeting	• Study one student's texts each day; pose questions to students to find out more information.	Same.
Word Wall	• Post words we can read in categories or genres.	Highlight adjectives, pronouns, etc.

Classroom library	• Add bins of everyday texts to explore and enjoy during independent reading. • Math extension - classify texts into categories like menus, shopping...	Study examples of informational versus fiction texts.
Embedded Sight Word minilessons	• Find examples of sight words. • Invite students to hunt for sight words in class library books.	

Figure 4.15 *(Cont.)*

Literacy Activity	Engagements to Explore at School	
	Kindergarten	1st–4th grade
Embedded phonics minilessons	• Develop long and short vowel or diphthong minilessons (e.g., *Ch* in "Cheerios")	Find prefixes and suffixes within everyday texts.
Writing letters, thank-you cards, etc.	• Use letter and notes from family to initiate letter writing.	Same.
Student of the week	• Family sends to school examples of what they read at home.	Family member sends to school examples of work-related reading and writing.

Literacy Activity	Engagements to Send Home to Families	
	Kindergarten	1st–4th grade
Literacy Book	• Every child chooses one everyday text; take photo of child with text and have child write about importance of everyday text in their life.	

Want to Know More?

- Visit Global Family Research Project (globalfrp.org).
- Study Whitmore and Wilson's (2016) "Photographs That Cracked Open Narrow Kindergarten Writing Practices for Children and Their Teacher."
- Examine Endrizzi's (2016) "Photos as Bridges into Hidden Literacy Lives."
- Explore this *Whooo's Reading* blog post, which features six helpful apps for photography with students: http://blog.whooosreading.org/photography-apps -and-ideas-for-the-classroom/.

---

discover how literacy is woven into the fabric of everyday life. Inviting families to become literacy informants elevates their desire to respect learning at school.

CHILDREN'S BOOKS

de la Peña, M. (2015). *Last stop on Market Street.* New York: G.P. Putnam's Sons.
Hoban, T. (1987). *I read signs.* New York: Greenwillow Books.
Jonas, A. (1992). *The 13th clue.* New York: Greenwillow Books.

APPENDIX 4.1

Appendix 4.1

Kindergarten Children's Books with Environmental and Recreational Text

---

AUTHOR AND TITLE	ESSENTIAL QUESTIONS TO SHARE DURING READ-ALOUDS	CLASSROOM CONNECTIONS
Reading in community Hoban, T. (1987). *I read signs*. New York: Greenwillow Books. de la Peña, M. (2016). *Last stop on Market Street*. New York: G.P. Putnam's Son. Milich, Z. (2005). *City signs*. Kids Can Press. *Signs in our world*. (2006). London: DK Children.	Can you find a sign we can read? Where can we find this sign? Who would read this sign? Why would someone read this sign? Let's think about someone in your family who would read this sign and why.	Create a Learning Center where readers can continue to investigate various children's books containing everyday texts and create a chart of texts and who might be reading. During independent reading time, invite readers to hunt through the class library for more books showing examples of everyday texts.

Reading at home
Jonas, A. (1992). *The 13th clue*. New York: Greenwillow Books.
Brandt, L. (2014). *Maddi's fridge*. Brooklyn, NY: Flashlight Press.

Where does this story take place?
Who is reading?
What are they reading?
Why are they reading?
Let's think about how you and your family members read at home.
Who can tell us about a time when someone in their family read the same text?

1st–4th Grade Children's Books with Environmental and Recreational Text

AUTHOR AND TITLE	ESSENTIAL QUESTIONS	CLASSROOM CONNECTIONS
Allen, S., & Landaman, J. (2006). *Read anything good lately?* Minneapolis: Millbrook. Allen, S., & Landaman, J. (2010). *Written anything good lately?* Minneapolis: Millbrook. Jacobs, J. D., & Swender, J. (2004). *My subway ride*. Salt Lake City: Gibbs Smith.	Begin by asking students to visualize all the moments they read that morning before coming to school. Create a class list of reading events and purposes for reading. Students can develop their own list and continue adding while the teacher shares the book. Who/what/why are these children and adults reading? Compare this reading event to experiences you have with your family. When has someone in your family read something similar?	Create a family project asking parents to help students record examples of family members reading and writing over several days. Explain project through family newsletter.

Chapter 5

Adapting Curriculum to Include Families' Ways of Knowing

GUIDING PRINCIPLE FOUR

Teachers can build bridges of understanding between home and school by building and expanding on curricular explorations and adapting them to the families' literacy events.

Jakub Oreziak returned to teach in the elementary school he attended as a youngster after graduating from one of the state colleges. He felt the pull back to his neighborhood as more and more Polish adults and their children settled in his town since May 2004, adding to the already high immigrant population of the school. The high unemployment rate and low wages after Poland's accession to the European Union created one of the largest waves of emigration.

His parents brought him to the United States in the 1990s, found jobs in the service industry, and learned English adequately enough to participate in everyday life. His parents did not leave the neighborhood often and left him to negotiate his studies and social life by himself. He understood what it was like to enter a new school in a new country with little knowledge of the English language. Although many of the new families from many different backgrounds had quickly acclimated to their new life in America and were financially secure, their lack of knowledge of the school system still baffled and frustrated them.

Jakub certainly felt like a high-iron man working on a bridge, trying to adapt what he felt was best for his students and what the families wanted of him for their children. He tried his best to help families understand the school system and the routines of his classroom. He was sensitive to the backgrounds of his students, especially those struggling with literacy acquisition. They presented many challenges he was ready to meet during his guided reading lessons, and he adapted curriculum in all the content areas. His family surveys had provided many opportunities to modify and enhance his lessons across all areas of study. His concern was with the work he sent home and the suggestions he made to families to support their children's literacy acquisition through authentic, family experiences.

The parents' request for worksheets (what he called "skill-and-drill exercises") and their desire to keep track of their children's work through the worksheets was frustrating. He wanted the parents to monitor the work he sent home, work with the children on completing assignments, and contribute their own literacy traditions. Homework is a very important aspect of the Polish educational system; parents are given a detailed timetable along with exercise books. Parents following the timetable can monitor their children's progress and can access the curriculum through the work brought home. They wanted their children, even those struggling with literacy, to receive and complete the same work required of all students. He found this to be true of many of families new to the educational system in which Jakub taught.

The difference between Jakub's school and classroom and the expectations of the majority of the families of the children was significant. He wanted to honor home literacy events, even when the families failed to see their importance in their children's learning. Not all activity needs to be about homework, but a great deal should be about learning and educational aspirations.

He felt this was exceptionally important for children for whom literacy acquisition seemed more challenging. He believed that parents were the first teachers and that activities at home, meals together, and participation in

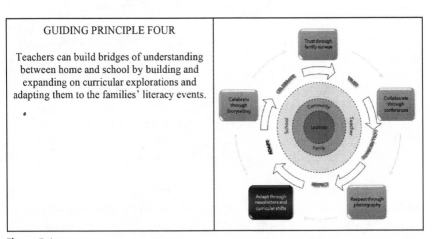

Figure 5.1.

family chores were important lessons on the value of learning. The parents of those students struggling with literacy, both English-language natives and emergent bilinguals, seemed to want more activities that would duplicate the work in school. They refused to see the value of their home activities and experiences and the suggestions he made that tapped into those family events. He needed to find a way to adapt and better explain his goals for family involvement toward enhanced literacy acquisition.

INSIGHTS FROM RESEARCH ON HOMEWORK

Jakub had not given too much thought to the type of homework families expected to find in their children's backpacks each night. He had not explored the current understanding of homework and its purpose or how it could be adapted and defined differently from classroom to classroom and school to school. He was determined to understand homework from a broad perspective in order to explain it properly to parents and to adapt homework to meet both parental and school expectations and requirements.

Kohn (2006) believes homework should be limited to those times when it seems appropriate and important. Corno (1996; cited in Kohn) states, "The best teachers vary their use of homework according to students' interests and capabilities. The sheer amount has little to no relation to any objective indicator of educational accomplishments" (p. 28). Homework assignments begin when teachers reflect on their knowledge of the curriculum and their understanding of the skills, abilities, and needs of their students and the characteristics and situations of the students' families. "Teachers have a responsibility to select and design assignments that are purposeful, engaging and high quality" (Epstein & VanVoorhis, 2001, p. 187).

This is true for students struggling with literacy achievement as well. When teachers assign students struggling with literacy acquisition less homework or less interesting homework, they convey to the students and their families low expectations (Epstein & VanVoorhis, 2001), and children who do less well at school receive more help from their parents (Silinskas, Niemi, Lerkkanen, & Nurmi, 2013).

The research on parental assistance with homework crosses both sides of the aisle. In examining homework assistance at home, Silinskas, Niemi, Lerkkanen, and Nurmi (2013) found that some studies have shown a positive relationship between the assistance students received at home and their achievement in elementary school. Yet they also found, "Homework assistance may also be detrimental for the evolving academic performance because it may lead the child to think negatively about his or her performance, which may then decrease skill development" (p. 45).

Similarly, Patall, Cooper, and Robinson (2008) found mixed findings conducting a meta-analysis of studies on parental involvement with homework. They found parental homework assistance accelerates learning, improves attitudes toward school, and facilitates communication between the child and parent and the teacher and the parent. However, they also found that parental assistance with homework can interfere with learning and can produce emotional costs such as tension, frustration, disappointment, and pressure to perform well. Strong parental assistance includes the development of cognitive, affective, and behavioral strategies such as goal setting, planning, time management, and attentiveness.

Low-performing children are more likely to receive parental assistance with homework. Their involvement with homework demonstrates their beliefs about schoolwork, homework, and learning. It is the quality of parental homework assistance that is important to children's academic development, not the frequency (Silinskas, Niemi, Lerkkanen, & Nurmi, 2013). Homework should be designed to promote child and family conversations that give opportunity to share ideas on what the child is learning and reinforce the importance of schoolwork.

Families need to understand the curricular objectives homework is designed to meet, especially homework designed for children struggling with literacy acquisition. Families of struggling readers and writers and their teachers need the opportunity to develop two-way communication around homework.

Homework can be a powerful tool for letting parents and other adults know what their children are learning, for giving children and families a reason to talk about what is going on at school, and for giving teachers the opportunity to hear from families about what children are learning (Walker, Dempsey-Hoover, Whetsel, & Green, 2004). This can occur when teachers invite families to be part of the process and to discuss positive ways homework assistance can happen. Parents know their child's strengths, learning styles, interests, and work preferences. Teachers can use this information to inform parents about homework assistance. See table 5.1 for advice in considering the roles of homework.

Suggestions for how to set a positive environment; guidelines for reinforcement and instruction; how to break large tasks into discrete, manageable parts; how to oversee, check, and reinforce efforts; how to help child focus; appropriate developmental expectations; and in general how to be helpful (Patall, Cooper, & Robinson, 2008; Walker, Dempsey-Hoover, Whetsel, & Green, 2004) are among some of the workshop ideas for teachers and schools to employ around homework. Teachers can also design web pages to provide general information to parents on how to be involved with homework as well as specific information about nightly homework assignments.

Table 5.1

Types of Homework		
Type	*Example*	*Considerations*
Reinforcement	Worksheets requiring students to practice the skills recently learned in school	Students successful at learning the skill will find the worksheet a page of practice. Students who were not successful at learning the skill will find it difficult and frustrating. Worksheets are not designed to teach.
Enrichment	Watching a television program together that was tied to the curriculum such as an episode of *Nova* or something on the History Channel	Not all families have the time to watch a program when it airs. Not all families are fluent in the language of the television program. When all family members can watch together, concepts from school can be enhanced and family members understand what is happening in class.
Extension	Visiting a local museum offering a show tied to the curriculum (for example, a local museum displaying the art of Eric Carle)	This can extend the school learning into other venues not easily accessible for students and their teachers. Personal conversations and connections can be made when families participate in a visit together. However, problems with availability or admission costs can be prohibitive.

Jakub began to think about ways he could share information, his beliefs, and school policy about homework with parents. He thought of ways he could use his classroom newsletter as a means of disseminating information and his thoughts about homework. He thought it might be a good idea to share information with parents at back-to-school nights.

INSIGHTS FROM RESEARCH ABOUT ADAPTING CURRICULAR EXPLORATIONS TO FAMILIES' LITERACY EVENTS

Jakub's experience with parents from other countries and those familiar with another educational system is not unique. The lack of knowledge between the two systems causes frustration and disappointment for families and teachers alike. The dissonance that may exist between values of education at home and at school needs to be acknowledged and straightened out. "Such lack of factual information may regard how the education system is set up and works in practice, what pedagogical values and reasoning lie behind different teaching methodologies and what assumption about children's learning and well-being supports certain practices with the two systems" (Ryndyk & Johannessen, 2015, p. 23).

In speaking of Latino families, Gaitan (2004) found that parents who had less experience with the school, had low academic attainment, or spoke limited English often found themselves even more isolated in a stressful situation like navigating a school system. So Jakub's insider information about the Polish community applies to other communities as well. The Polish and many other educational systems are uniform and centralized, so individual schools have less autonomy. There is less emphasis on choice. All children, regardless of their achievements, must adhere to the same objectives and level of accomplishment.

Parents of children struggling to achieve literacy competency do not want them to receive different or special homework. In addition, in many cultures, connotations about a student's disability or academic struggle are a barrier to collaboration (Miller & Nguyen, 2014). The child struggling in school is often seen as a poor reflection on the family. Miller and Nguyen (2014) suggest educating parents about the school system and pointing out similarities and differences to increase understanding.

Tejero-Hughes, Valle-Riestra, and Arguelles (2008) found families wanted the school to provide them with specific strategies to support their children, identified as having academic challenges, at home. What teachers want to do is build on family strengths to reinforce classroom learning. The family is the child's first teacher. The moment-to-moment experiences in running a home; the stories told in a car ride, on the bus, across the table over a meal; doing chores—all reveal the importance of education and values of learning. In many cases, the viewpoint of the family runs parallel with the school's expectations.

Early exposure to a variety of literacy activities that families provide are beneficial to children (Dail & Payne, 2010). "Home literacy activities provide a framework for observing parents as educators in their natural milieu" (Gaitan, 2004, p. 53). Tredway (2003; cited in Dunsmore, Ordonez-Jasis, & Herrera, 2013) suggests using community mapping, typically used in fields like environmental science or sociology, as an inquiry-based method the teacher can use to understand and change his or her perspective on the family from outsider to insider. This approach allows teachers to attach meaning to language and literacy practices of the home, allowing for out-of-school literacy activities to support school-based practices.

Dunsmore, Ordonez-Jasis, and Herrera (2013) suggest using information gathered from family surveys (similar to those mentioned in chapter 2), interviews, artifacts, and recorded and documented observations of family and community events and deeply reflecting on these data to understand the patterns, themes, and relationships the children experience in and out of school. By thinking broadly about school curriculum and familial and community events, teachers can design family activities that enhance school-based knowledge and are tailored to the individual literacy strengths and vulnerabilities of the child.

As Dunsmore, Ordonez-Jasis, and Herrera (2013) found, community mapping allowed events that "create a learning space in which motivation and engagement were high and the literacy practices surrounding the event captured students emotionally as well as intellectually" (p. 337). At-home activities that intentionally connect the two worlds children experience can be powerful motivators, acknowledge family literacy practices, and strengthen student learning.

Family interests and experiences can be used as recommendations to families to build continuity between school and home activities. Teachers can suggest home literacy activities that not only enhance the school curriculum but are culturally relevant, are tailored to the current literacy strengths of the student and the family, and can be woven into the family's present experiences.

Jakub did not want to get lost in the clouds and disappear like the ironworker on the bridge. He began to record what he was specifically learning about the children in his classroom and their personal family histories, looking for patterns of information in order to design instructional opportunities, suggest home literacy activities, and find ways to share the information with parents.

Teacher Connection

Tamara supports a family with homework:

Yesenia's family came from the Dominican Republic and her cousin joined them a month later. Both parents speak English, but their way of approaching school is very different. They don't really feel that it's their obligation to do homework with the children or to get involved with their education. I kept trying to reach out to them. I wrote notes and letters, called on the phone, even the administration tried to reach out. I'd catch them outside, but I found out they weren't comfortable with reading and writing. Finally, I had them come in; I modeled how to do the homework with their children. At first they were apprehensive and they looked a little uncomfortable, but I invited their daughter to join us. I said, "Show me how we do it in class." After a while we were all doing it together. That helped me this year. When the child did it in front of the parent, and then the mother saw how easy it was, she realized she didn't have to read the story. That was a successful story for me! I also modified the child's homework because it had to be a little bit less; it had to be different.

3, 2, 1 STOP AND THINK

3. **Identify three** new insights you have about homework.
2. **Brainstorm two** ways you can modify your homework assignments to better support your struggling readers.
1. **Create one** letter to families to explain your view of homework.

ADAPTING FOR FAMILY INVOLVEMENT
IN LEARNING ACTIVITIES

The goal is for teachers to provide information on how to involve families in their children's learning outside of the classroom. As Battle-Bailey (2004) states, "Fostering social interactions is crucial for developing an understanding of reading activities" (p. 37). Teachers should strive to connect classroom activities to real-world activities related to the students' home lives, making school work more meaningful and relevant.

Holmes (2011) found that while parents wanted to be involved with their children's learning and informed about their children's progress, it was not always clear—particularly for parents of children struggling with literacy—how they might go about it. Teachers need to create forums for information sharing about strategies for helping children read at home. Many families believe that an effective at-home reading program is one that duplicates in-school instruction.

Information about the reading process and effective strategies parents can employ at home may clear up any misconceptions and inadequate assumptions about parental roles in at-home reading. Hornsby (2000) states, "the main aim of the 'take-home' reading program is that children will share positive reading experiences with other people who are significant in their lives" (p. 49). Parents can be encouraged to form book clubs with their children around authors, genres, and topics reflecting the interests of the child.

Learning what practices are important without interrupting the authentic interactions around books at home should be the goal of an at-home reading program. Book selection strategies, communicating and questioning strategies about reading, how and when to correct miscues or encourage word identification strategies, as well as other topics can be shared with families of children struggling with literacy acquisition.

Giving important information is not enough. "Parents need to be offered support in understanding how they can use the suggestions" (DeFauw & Burton, 2009, p. 36). Goldberg (2001) states, "Parents' beliefs about literacy will influence how they use materials and engage in literacy instruction with children" (p. 223). If parents value phonics-based instruction more than just reading, they teach decoding with materials sent home rather than focusing on comprehension.

Herold (2011) suggests there is a correlation between a teacher's theoretical understanding of reading acquisition and learning and the instructional approach they choose. This is especially true for teachers of struggling readers. The assumptions teachers make about their students struggling with literacy acquisition influence the way they encourage parents to engage with their children in literacy activities at home.

There are also assumptions families have about struggling readers. The need to create positive, successful opportunities around reading, especially at home, cannot be minimized. "Teaching for success includes building on what is known, that is, starting from the child's strengths" (Herold, 2011, p. 45). The "Unit Tune-Up: Teacher Tool" found in appendix 5.1 can be used to examine your own unit plan to reflect on the materials, curricula interconnections, avenues for learning tailored for struggling readers, and opportunities for families as learning partners.

Effective teachers communicate and empower parents of struggling readers about ways to engage their children at home in literacy activities different from those in school yet supportive of learning. "The intent of parent education is to empower families through information and resources so they can play active roles in their child's educational planning and delivery" (Mueller, 2014, p. 8). Workshops on these topics may reduce the stress and frustration many families feel when trying to understand and help their children struggling with literacy acquisition. Jakub began thinking of family gatherings to increase awareness of educational expectations and the activities and opportunities for families to be involved.

Teacher Connection

Frank describes the use of an online program to support bilingual learners at home:

In our school we have a few students who are ELLs, and their parents speak primarily, almost exclusively, Spanish. English is a language barrier. So we use a program called Achieve3000, which is an online differentiated reading program and it's offered in English and Spanish. A great tool I've used, especially with ELLs who struggle with literacy, are bilingual books or books available in both English and Spanish. We read the stories in English in school and give them access to the same book in Spanish at home. In this way we bridge back and forth since families can have a conversation about books being read in school and get involved in their children's learning.

Newsletters

According to McCarthy (2000), a key component in creating home–school communication appears to be the sharing of information. Jakub employed a monthly classroom newsletter to establish a two-way communication avenue with families of children in his class. Through the newsletter, he could proactively share information about strategies and topics taught in class as well as suggestions for parents. Home activities, websites, television programs, museum displays, or other places of interest coordinated to monthly themes were included in the newsletters. Yet Jakub's newsletter was also designed to draw out parents with knowledge or experience in the topics or themes being studied, acknowledging them as valuable contributors to their children's learning.

Not all families have the time to attend family workshops. The newsletter helps parents feel connected to the classroom. By sharing with families topics being discussed in school, families can have specific conversations about life in the classroom. Students benefit from a more personalized curriculum. With information on websites, book lists, community resources, and activities to enhance classroom learning, parents can tailor their home events to match their lifestyle and children's interests and level of literacy acquisition while supporting the classroom curriculum.

In one newsletter Jakub asked families to create time lines and illustrate them with drawings, photographs, and written explanations. He learned about each student's life, discovered important cultural holidays and traditions, and gained a broader awareness of their backgrounds. He used Google Translate to make his newsletter available in multiple languages and posted these on his classroom website and encouraged his students to share them with their families.

The template found in appendix 5.2 offers a way to begin your own classroom newsletter. As you employ a monthly newsletter, you will find other topics and areas you will want to include. A common complaint from teachers is they find the newsletters at the bottom of backpacks, never given to the families of their students. Seesaw (web.seesaw.me) is a free website to upload newsletters, photos, videos, drawings, PDFs, and links. The site states that it "empowers students to independently document what they are learning in school." By using this or another website to electronically deliver newsletters

---

Teacher Connection

Alice's newsletter practices:

I send home weekly newsletters. Each newsletter outlines the teaching points for the week. I also create photo albums biweekly that I put on our class website. Each photo album includes different charts for the week (allowing parents to mirror my language), whole group activities, and pictures of children collaborating in different areas.

as well as other messages to families, you are assured of not finding crumbled newsletters at the bottom of backpacks.

Using Technology

When parents and children use technology at home, it is usually done for a specific purpose. The authentic events around computer usage at home provide opportunities for struggling readers and their families to engage in literacy. Emailing friends and relatives provides children with a written venue for two-way communication. Children, with their family members, can research areas of interest or topics related to school-based learning in a variety of subjects.

Looking up recipes, discovering answers to curiosities, and finding information about products, online ordering, and movie timetables all contribute to struggling readers' engagement with literacy practices. Online texts and ebooks, or talking electronic books, are often motivating and give control to struggling readers and their families.

Websites

A number of books written for children have websites connected to the author or the book itself. The pages are not only designed for teachers but for children and their families, offering suggestions and serving as a springboard into family literacy experiences around favorite books, authors, and interests. Websites often include conversation starters or open-ended questions that can be used to guide families into more authentic talks about the books they are reading together.

Children interested in current events can go to www.weeklyreaders.com to find articles. There are also games to play and activities, all of which children and families can complete together. Newsela.com requires teachers and students to sign up for a free account using their school email. Newsela gives access to articles on a number of subjects, tailored by grade level, in English and Spanish. ReadWorks.org also requires students and educators to sign up for its free service, which gives access to articles by grade level. With each article, the lexile and curriculum standards met are provided.

Candlewick Press just developed an online book club that can be accessed at www.myfirstbookclub.com. They have handpicked titles for early readers and customized resources to deepen children's engagement with books. Initially, they offer four different books, activities to go along with the books, and questions to start conversations about the books being read. This may be a good place for families to start their own book clubs at home. Many parents do not know how to start conversations with their children or to design activities to go along with the books. This site provides a beginning for many families.

Almost all authors have websites. Many of children's favorite books can be found on YouTube being read by the author or someone else. Laura

Numeroff's website (www.LauraNumeroff.com) has many links to her books, including a thirty-five-minute live story time. The website www .mousecookiebooks.com has links to characters from Numeroff's books and activities, recipes, and games coordinated to *If You Give a Mouse a Cookie* and other If You Give … books.

Mercer Mayer has over 170 Little Critter books. The website www .littlecritter.com offers coloring pages, activities, apps, and videos of Mayer reading his books.

Older children are reading books like *Wonder* by R. J. Palacio, a book all families could read together and one that demands conversations. By using a search engine and entering the book title and author, many sites come up, many appropriate for the classroom but many for guidance in talking about the book. One helpful search engine for older readers is Goodreads.com, a website that suggests titles, text sets, and other genres based on a user's search. The site also enables users to create a personalized account that saves read texts, encourages readers to write reviews, and connects readers to user communities organized by genre, author, or theme-based groupings.

Games

Holmes (2011) found parents spoke positively about the learning benefits of games used with their children, including the support they gave to their children's learning, their affirmative and formative feedback, and the focus games provided for discussion about literacy. "In particular, all of the parents were pleased to have been able to use games derived from a literacy intervention they knew to be well regarded at school—they did not need to be literacy experts" (p. 13). They also appreciated that the design of the games met their children's specific learning needs without being babyish, a common complaint about games for struggling readers.

We have used many games with our struggling readers in our after-school program. Many are purchased from companies manufacturing commercially prepared games designed to address specific areas of the reading process. We found popular board games such as *Totally Gross Science* and card games such as *Apples to Apples* to be extremely popular with the struggling readers with whom we work. Each game demands reading for understanding and implementing that information to play effectively to "win" the game. Games can be found at popular toy stores and teacher stores such as Lakeshore.

In addition, the tutors in our program have constructed games based on the interests and assessment information gathered during the tutoring process. The games constructed should be built around student interests and strengths and serve as an intervention measure. Games should be simple enough to play with another child and the child's family. We have found both board games and card games very popular with students and their families.

The game found in appendix 5.3 was designed for a boy interested in baseball. Many of the rules of baseball were built into the rules of the game. For example, one player may not pass another player along the baseline. The game cards for this particular game were designed to increase writing ability, reading ability, and other areas of language arts. One card asked the child to take out a piece of writing he was working on and to circle three nouns. Then he was asked to come up with "rich" adjectives for each. The timer in the game was used, limiting the amount of time the child could spend answering the command on the game card. Some game cards asked for information about specific players, causing the student to use his computer and look up information. The baseball board game can be adapted to other curriculum areas and at other levels since game cards can easily be added or replaced.

The Go Fish card game found in appendix 5.4 can be made for word study. Go Fish uses fifty-two playing cards, making up thirteen sets of four cards each. The idea of the game is to collect all four cards within a set to make a match. When all cards have been played, the winner is the one who has collected the most matches. Consider making up a set of cards with initial or final consonants, short or long vowel sounds, digraphs, blends, or word families. The cards should be clearly recognizable and able to be categorized into the game's focus.

We have also hosted a games night, inviting families to play games the tutors have constructed for their children as well as commercially prepared games. We send the games home with the families for future play. We ask the children in our program to design and write their own invitations to their families. The invitations include the date, time, and location and invite everyone to bring a snack. When families are not in a position to bring snacks to share, we provide the snacks for the event.

SUMMARY

In this chapter, we examined attitudes about homework and encouraged you to take a look at your own homework practices and the expectations families of struggling readers have about the homework assigned to their children. We then explored the research on adapting literacy curriculum to family literacy events. Practical ways, based on theoretical implications, for involving families in their children's learning outside the classroom were offered, specifically the use of newsletters, technology, websites, and games.

Want to Know More?

To further think about homework and literacy learning outside of school, consult the following:

- Kohn (2006), "Abusing Research: The Study of Homework and Other Examples."
- Kreider, Caspe, and Hiatt-Michael (2013), *Promising Practices for Engaging Families in Literacy.*
- Free newsletter templates from Lucidpress.com: https://www.lucidpress.com/pages/templates/newsletters/school-newsletters.
- IXL Language Arts for at-home support with literacy skills: https://www.ixl.com/ela/.
- Crash Course and Crash Course Kids for at-home support to build content knowledge across disciplines: https://www.youtube.com/user/crashcourse/featured and https://www.youtube.com/user/crashcoursekids.

CHILDREN'S BOOKS

Numeroff, L. J. (2015). *If you give a mouse a cookie.* New York: HarperCollins.
Palacio, R. J. (2012). *Wonder.* New York: Knopf Books for Young Readers.

APPENDIX 5.1

Appendix 5.1

Unit Tune-Up: Teacher Tool

Use this graphic organizer to …
1. Organize a unit's content and materials
2. Reflect on how the unit's content and materials connect to families' backgrounds, interests, and literacy routines

---

Unit Title:

Unit Component	Guiding Question	Additions/Refinements	Action Step
Content	*How does the content of this unit reflect students' backgrounds, interests, and needs?*		
Materials	*How do the materials in this unit scaffold and support understanding of its content for struggling readers?*		

Instructional Activities/ Routines	*How do the activities/ routines in this unit provide access points for struggling readers?*
Technology	*How does technology connect struggling readers and families to the unit's content?*
Cross-Content Connections	*How does the unit create connections to other content areas, such as science, social studies, or mathematics? Where are there entry points that could be adapted to struggling readers?*
Opportunities to Build Motivation and Engagement	*What kinds of opportunities have been included to foster motivation and engagement with students and families?*

Title of Your Newsletter
Date of your Newsletter

Greeting from the Teacher

This short column should be written in a warm and respectful manner. It sets the tone for the rest of the newsletter. Alert them to upcoming events, thank them for their support and help for certain projects, or tell them what to expect this month. Here you start to develop trust.

Dates to Remember

Dates for school photos, field trips, back-to-school nights, conferences, and school holidays for the month should be listed here.

If something extraordinary is happening the next month, you might want to include it in this list.

You can bullet these items or list them one under the other.

This Month's Websites

Share the school website or your own classroom website address here. You might also list the website for the location of a class trip or sites you found that would enhance instruction and parents and children could navigate together. For example, when doing an author study, list the author's website, or if you are studying the planets, websites for further investigation could be listed. It is here that ideas for adapting the curriculum can be shared.

> We Need Your
> Help This Month.

This is your chance to get the families involved in the life of your classroom. Perhaps you are studying time lines in social studies and math. You can invite families to create their own family time line to be shared in class. Give them the opportunity to include photographs or to bring in objects. This part of your newsletter helps with collaboration.

Look What We Did!

Share the work that your students completed during the previous month, especially work that you had mentioned in the newsletter. Families are more apt to read the newsletter and children are more apt to share the newsletter with their parents if their work is included. Scan it in, type in comments made by the children, or include photographs of bulletin boards with their work. In this way the newsletter becomes a vehicle for communication. Sharing work with families shows the respect you have for them and their children.

Drawing Families Out

In this section of the newsletter you want to draw out families with knowledge or experience in the topics or themes being studied. By inviting those families into the classroom to share their knowledge and experiences, you acknowledge them as valuable contributors to their children's learning. This helps with trust, collaboration, respect, and celebration.

Common family practices that support the topics and themes can be mentioned here. For example, when studying fairy tales, invite families to share the ones they tell or read at home with the class. This is a way

Figure 5.2. Newsletter

to celebrate the differences among families.

Units of Study

Using subheadings, share with the families the topics and activities the children in your class will be involved in during the month. Be clear about your learning objectives for the month and how homework helps support these objectives. What books will they be reading? Will they be participating in literature circles? If so, tell the families about them. What will they be learning in science? Mathematics? Social studies? Art? What special skills or strategies will they be mastering this month? Give specific ways parents can help.

Invite Feedback

Find a way for feedback. This could be a simple note or family journal entry about a family–child activity tried out at home, a book they shared, a trip they took, or a response to an invitation made by you to help in the classroom. You are letting them know they are important, which builds trust and respect.

Add graphics to your newsletter and when possible photographs from your classroom, those sent in by families as they have engaged in literary events, and children's work whenever possible. When mentioning books for adaptation, websites for collaboration, or any other material and resources, you want to make sure that the range is inclusive to all students in your classroom. Families can access those that are most appropriate to their struggling readers.

Figure 5.2 (*Cont.*)

APPENDIX 5.3 BASEBALL GAME

Goal of the Game: To have your team score more runs than the other team

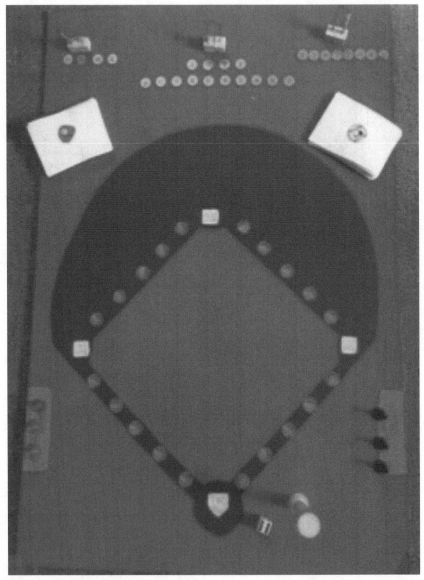

Figure 5.3.   Baseball Game

Game Pieces:

6 "men"—3 for each team
2 counters to keep track of runs
1 counter to keep track of outs
One die
One timer

Game cards—two sets:

Baseball-marked cards for each pitch
Mitt-marked cards or challenge cards for the bases

How to Play:

1. Each team has three players. Place them in their dugout.
2. Decide how many innings you will play.
3. Roll the die, and the highest roll becomes the visiting team and is at bat first.
4. Put your first player at home plate and draw a baseball-marked card. If you answer the question correctly, roll the die and move your player the corresponding number of spaces or balls on the game board. If you fail to answer the question correctly, back to the dugout—you are out.
5. Put the next player at home plate and repeat instructions from above. Or if you have a player along the baseline, you can choose to move that player around the baseline before putting another player on the field. There are advantages to having multiple players on the field.
6. With each roll of the die, you may choose to move any of your players.
7. Continue moving up to three players around the bases. Each time a player crosses home plate move your team counter to score a run.
8. If a player lands on first, second, or third base, draw a mitt-marked card and follow the instructions. If you answer correctly, move according to the card. (See special rules below.) If you fail to answer the challenge correctly, you are out and must move your piece back to the dugout.
9. After three outs, the other team takes the field.

Special Rules of Play and Things to Consider

One player may not move ahead of another player on the baseline. If you roll the die and it forces you to pass another player, it is an out and the player goes back to the dugout.

If your player lands on the same space as another player, the player is out and goes back to the dugout.

When on base and completing a mitt card, all players on the board may move ahead. For example, if you are on first base and score a double, you may move the player on first to third, and any other players on the board will also move ahead. Or if you have a player on first and third and score a single, you might want to move the player on third base home to score a run. Likewise, if you complete a mitt card for a home run and have a player in the dugout, you can move that player around the bases and any other players on the board will also score. After completing a mitt card, your next turn will be a baseball card.

APPENDIX 5.4 GO FISH CARD GAME

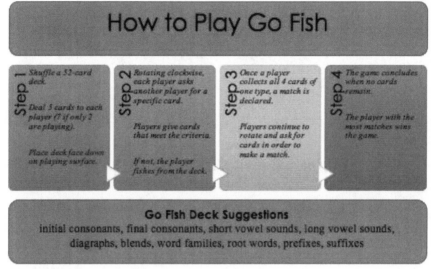

Figure 5.4.   Go Fish Card Game

To play Go Fish, first shuffle the deck of fifty-two cards and deal five cards to each player (seven cards if only two are playing). Put the remaining cards face down in the middle of the table.

Moving clockwise from the dealer, players in turn ask another player of their choosing if they have a certain specific type of card. For example, "Jenny, do you have any words with a short *i*? If the player does, the player gives any and all cards with words with a short *i* to the asking player. The asking player may take another turn and continue to take a turn asking the same or other players for other specific cards. If at any time a player does not have a card asked for, the player responds, "Go fish!" and that player picks a card up from the pile and their turn is over.

When a player collects all four cards of one type, it is declared a match and the cards are put in front of the player.

If a player runs out of cards while the game is still in play, the player draws five cards from the pile on the table. If there are fewer than five cards in the pile, the player will take the remainder of them.

The game continues until all players are out of cards. The player with the most matches wins the game.

Chapter 6

Celebrating Literacy through Sharing Stories

> **GUIDING PRINCIPLE FIVE**
>
> Teachers can build bridges of understanding between home and school by recognizing and celebrating families' cultural diversity through building on the power of storytelling and family stories.

Rosina, a petite eight-year-old, long hair braided expertly, stood nervously at the door to her third grade classroom. Her classmates ran about the classroom as Jessica Murray, their teacher, directed them in setting up tables and chairs. It was the second publishing party for the third grade. Her friends were excited about sharing their informational books with their families. Yet Rosina remembered, with embarrassment, the first time her mom came to a school event. Unlike most of the other parents, her mom sat along the edge of the classroom and watched rather than walking around the room to read the books and write comments. She was sure some of the kids were giggling when her mother greeted Ms. Murray in Spanish.

Born in the Dominican Republic, Rosina traveled to the United States with her family when she was three. Her family emigrated to the large northeastern city to join cousins who ran a small dry-cleaning store. Through a community-based program designed to jump-start the educational achievement of recent immigrants, Rosina received a scholarship to attend a private school several miles (or many subway stops) away from her primarily Hispanic neighborhood.

Rosina's parents, Silvio and Marta, believed this was a unique opportunity for their daughter. They wanted Rosina to graduate from high school, attend college, and enjoy a professional career. The rumors that they'd heard about the local schools frightened them; a private school in a different area of the city appeared to be a better choice for Rosina. Marta spoke Spanish at home, and whenever they had to come to school Rosina served as the translator. Rosina didn't enjoy this role.

She found it difficult to continually be the translator for her mother and sometimes was embarrassed that her mother and her teacher couldn't talk. She noticed that when other parents dropped their kids off in the playground they hung around talking with each other, while Rosina's mom rushed off.

Rosina's teacher, Jessica Murray, knew that Rosina and another student, Alex, came to the progressive private school through a scholarship program from a community-based organization and that their cultural, linguistic, and economic profiles differed from those of her primarily upper-middle-class, European American students. Although she considered herself an experienced teacher, Jessica primarily had worked with students and families like herself. While the progressive ethos of the school embraced diversity in its vision, mission, and brochures, in practice Jessica found she was left on her own to figure out what that meant in her third grade classroom with Rosina, Alex, and their families.

One of the unique features of the school was an integrated, thematic approach to curriculum. Social studies, in particular, played a focal role. Teachers like Jessica were expected to use social studies topics to integrate math, literacy, science, and arts. Her traditional teacher education training, in a small suburban college, had prepared her to teach the curriculum but not think beyond the disciplinary walls. For third grade, the social studies theme addressed was immigration. It was here she began to consider how she might create a thematic unit that could include all the disciplines and potentially be more inclusive of all her students. She began to investigate fiction and non-fiction tales on movement and change.

During the first weeks of school, Jessica assessed her students' reading and writing using the school's portfolio approach. This included running records of trade books, writing samples, conference notes, and interest surveys. Through these portfolios, Jessica learned not only about her students' reading and writing behaviors but about her students' interests. Rosina's performance on the reading assessments placed her several levels below the school's expectation for third grade.

With further analysis, Jessica determined that while Rosina decoded the text accurately, her comprehension wasn't as strong. The same held true for her writing. Each word was accurately spelled, but it appeared that Rosina only selected words that she could spell. Jessica winced when she

GUIDING PRINCIPLE FIVE Teachers can build bridges of understanding between home and school by recognizing and celebrating families' cultural diversity through building on the power of storytelling and family stories.	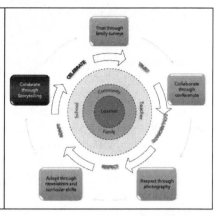

Figure 6.1

remembered how difficult it was to extract anything from Rosina for the first writing unit, which was a personal narrative. Even the "published" story, a story about a birthday party at a cousin's house, was difficult. Jessica understood that Rosina was a bilingual student who spoke English at school and Spanish at home. But Jessica did not want to see Rosina fall behind in her reading and writing development and wondered how her parents could help her if they didn't speak English.

Jessica's question is illustrative of the need for more attention to the linguistic and narrative strengths that are present in all families. As discussed in chapters 2 and 4, it is important to look beyond differences as deficits to view diversity as an asset. In this final principle, we bring together these principles as one of celebration.

Our fifth and final principle states: *Teachers can build bridges of understanding between home and school by recognizing and celebrating families' cultural diversity through building on the power of storytelling and family stories.*

INSIGHTS FROM RESEARCH INTO STORYTELLING

Family Stories in School Settings

Linda Winston in *Keepsakes: Using Family Stories in Elementary Classrooms* (1997) defines family stories, drawing from Zeitlin, as "any incident retold by one family about another over a period of years," but she goes on to expand on this definition, stating, "My definition also includes cautionary tales, folk tales, fairy tales, and the kinds of bedtime stories some parents make up for their young children each night, based on a recounting of a child's day. Family expressions, sayings, customs, keepsakes, photographs, recipes, holidays and celebrations also belong here" (p. 3).

Winston highlights teachers who make family stories the centerpiece of elements of their curriculum. One teacher creates a family study unit that includes letter writing between students and family members, developing interview skills that students use to create an oral history of an elder family member. Another invited family members to share their stories of coming to America as part of a third grade unit on immigration.

A fifth grade teacher incorporates family photo albums to support critical questions and analysis in a study of early twentieth-century immigration. Through these classroom vignettes, we see stories bridging classroom and home to create powerful learning opportunities. Family stories reflect our strengths, our struggles. Family stories are about people, places, events related to family and ancestors. They are a kind of passed-on family heirloom, which make each of us unique and part of a larger whole.

More recently, Cunningham (2015) reminds us that "we live in a world of stories" (p. 1) and argues that children's stories should take a prime place in elementary classrooms. She warns that with increasing attention to accountability measures, the opportunities for students and teachers, and we would add families, to share stories is diminished. Stories, both read and told, "encourage the children in our lives to become empathetic, caring people and more committed learners" (p. 18). Further, "I position story as alive and vital to the work we do with young people for them to read and keep reading stories in print and digital spaces, to engage in trust falls again and again and find their inky courage, and to be wide awake to the stories and issues around them" (p. 19). Access to stories, personal and through children's literature (see chapter 7 for more extensive discussion), is essential for children's literacy engagement. Aukerman (2015) states,

> Every meaning a child constructs for a text is, in some important way, a reflection of who s/he is. And valuing children for who they are and for what they bring into the classroom as learners—what I call a transformative perspective—means respecting and welcoming the full range of knowledge and practices they draw upon, including their meaning-making repertoires. (p. 55)

We would add that family stories are an essential part of who children are and what they bring to the classroom. For many children who struggle with reading, telling stories is a critical first and motivating step in developing a genuine connection to reading.

Here is an example of such an impact. Whitmore and Norton-Meier (2008) write about the power of a parent coming into school and telling a story. They relate the account of Pearl, a mom of a struggling student who comes into school to share a story of his difficult medical conditions at birth. For his classmates, this provides a context and narrative that fosters empathy. She also shared a children's story she wrote based on her experiences. John, her son, enjoyed the attention, and Pearl developed a new appreciation for his classmates and teacher. She became more comfortable with the school and focused on collaboration with his teachers. Importantly, John is also more motivated to read and write and, with this added support, demonstrates improvement.

The Significance of Storytelling

Storytelling enables learners and families to ...

- Create or share contexts for situations or events
- Engage with story elements through oral discussion of people (characters), events (plot), and place (setting)
- Celebrate memories
- Develop empathy

3, 2, 1 STOP AND THINK

   3. List three words you think of when you think of storytelling.
   2. Ask yourself two questions about how to engage and celebrate families through storytelling.
   1. Write one sentence that describes your understanding of the importance of storytelling.

Storytelling as a Universal Practice

Miller and Pennycuff (2008) define storytelling as "relating a tale to one or more listeners through voice and gesture. There is a critical social element in storytelling, the relationship between the listener and the speaker. It is related to the theatre, and with an aim of 'transporting' through time and space" (p. 37). Sipe (2008) identifies several key characteristics of storytelling, an oral performance (p. 217):

1. There is a flexibility in telling the story. Stories are not told "word for word" each time.
2. The storyteller acknowledges and adjusts to the reactions of the audience.
3. The success of the storytelling depends upon the relationship, developed through the experience between storyteller and audience.

4. In some cultures, storytelling is connected to other forms such as dance and visual arts, making it a multimedia experience.

Several researchers (Cliatt & Shaw, 1988; Isbell, Sobol, Lindauer, & Lowrance, 2004; Mello, 2001) highlight ways storytelling can support literacy instruction, especially in supporting comprehension. These researchers draw attention to unique attributes of storytelling such as attention to visualization since there are no pictures, inferencing from the vocal cues and gestures of the storyteller, high levels of engagement, and empathy.

Eder (2007) documented and analyzed Navajo storytelling practices and describes how stories are used to explain and transmit important cultural concepts. She notes the importance of families in continuing the traditions of storytelling.

From an Australian context, Fleer and Williams-Kennedy (2002) describe how teachers and Aboriginal families worked to learn more about cultural and social demands, traditions, and stories, an example of oral language being essential in maintaining tradition. Similarly, McKeough and colleagues (2008) argue that Aboriginal children benefit from school literacy programs that build on the strengths of their home oral storytelling traditions.

Ordonez-Jasis and Flores (2011) describe the importance of family retellings of ghost and mystery stories in a Mexican American community and, even more so, lullabies and other songs. They share that when educators heard parents share the songs, they recognized powerful emotions evoked by these memories. They write, "As the teachers carefully listened to the stories of the families and reflected upon the richness of literacy practices they found in the homes, a heightened consciousness soon developed as they came to rediscover and better appreciate the benefits of home-based stories and songs in the emergent literacy process" (p. 130). Unfortunately, some teachers may not have the opportunity to reflect on the role family stories and songs play in developing the literacy identities of their students, especially those struggling with literacy acquisition. Murillo (2012) explores the out-of-school literacies of bilingual children in southeast Texas. She finds that teachers ignore the importance of culturally specific oral language traditions: "Without knowledge of such examples, it is all too easy for teachers to 'underestimate' the literacies of Spanish-speaking families based on a deficit view that 'Mexicans don't read or write'" (p. 22).

This view only contributes to the deficit view of families. When this is the view of teachers and the school, families are not aware of their potential strengths and resources in supporting their children. If parents don't see their family stories as rich literacy experiences, it is imperative for teachers to support and encourage their family expertise.

Importance of Narrative Thinking

Narrative abilities are the expressive language used to describe things, relate events in order, and retell stories. These abilities develop far before children arrive at school and continue to be supported by families. For example, children first learn names of things, such as when a dad says, "See the dog?" or "Here comes the bus!" As children grow older, parents may, without thinking about it, support vocabulary development. A child, noticing a poster for a movie, asks her mom, "Why are they wearing spotted clothes?" to which the mom replies, "They are wearing camouflage, clothes to make them look like the animals and trees."

Further development grows with following directions or retelling stories. Children come to school with understanding of stories or narratives, and their "ways of telling stories are learned through observing and participating in narrative practices in their families" (Genishi & Dyson, 2009). Bruner (1986) reminds us that narrative thinking is a unique way of thinking and making sense of the world.

Yet stories, and the narrative discourses associated with them, may not play a primary role in classroom discourse. Educators (e.g., Hicks, 1998; Chang- Wells & Wells, 1992; Zigo, 2001) suggest that it is important for teachers to identify, draw upon, and integrate children's narrative discourses. "When teachers encourage students' natural inclinations toward narrative forms of meaning, in conjunction with text-based lessons, the students appear more engaged with textual content and demonstrate less resistance to reading material that might otherwise be challenging or frustrating" (Zigo, 2001, p. 64).

Developing Oral Language

Children come to school with oral language abilities, fostered by their families. The relationship between oral language development and reading development is strong. It is also a relationship that offers multiple opportunities for families to engage with their struggling reader. Reese, Suggate, Long, and Schaughency (2010) found that strong oral narrative skills predicted strong reading abilities. "The oral narrative variable that was most strongly correlated with early reading skill was the measure of narrative quality, not story memory" (p. 636). More specifically, a child's ability to introduce characters, use time, and identify cause and effect as he or she tells a story supports their reading development. This research suggests that storytelling, not only vocabulary use (Hart & Risley, 1995), supports children's reading development.

The role of storytelling as a family support is underappreciated but critically important. Reese, Sparks, and Leyva (2010) in their review of parent interventions for preschool language and literacy found that storytelling is a promising intervention for all types of families because "parents in a diverse range of cultures talk with children about past events" (p. 109). Interventions that included "increasing parents' use of open-ended questions during past narrative, particularly the use of 'where' and 'when' questions" (p. 109) increased children's performances on vocabulary measures. What's more, researchers found that a year after the intervention, children whose parents participated told narratives that were richer in descriptive language than those who had not.

For families of young readers, engaging in conversations to increase oral language is critical. The development of phonological awareness, that is, the ability to hear, identify, and change sounds in language, is a key component of early reading. Reese and colleagues (2015) describe this:

> One feature of the implicit sound talk was its playful quality. When parents used this strategy, it was not in a "teaching" tone of voice; instead, they adopted a playful, light tone to gently point out the sound features of the objects (e.g., *Does the brown banana have a beak?*). We suspect that the fun, playful nature of these comments is critical in the link to young children's phonological awareness. This information should be useful in designing interventions to help parents enhance their preschool children's phonological awareness. Playful, enjoyable activities for parent and child alike could be designed to help foster these skills. (p. 64)

These oral language activities are not only important for young children. Reese (2013) suggests that children of parents who learn to reminisce, sharing colorful and detailed retellings of family experiences, are better able to empathize with others' thoughts and emotions, which enables them to better perform in complex reading tasks. Storytelling, she argues, is "portable" and trainable.

While parents of young children readily ask questions to get children to elaborate on sentences—such as when a child says, "Dog out," a parent may extend the story to say, "Yes, Fido went out to the backyard"—we need to remember that all children benefit from questions to build their storytelling skills. Preteens and adolescents can retell the events of a personal story but benefit from adults' understanding in putting stories in perspective and relating them to larger issues and struggles.

Storytelling as Instructional Bridge between Home and School

Storytelling helps children make a connection between home and school, and teachers can extend that bridge to their families. Craig, Hull, Haggart, and Crowder (2001) outline several key features that support this view. First, storytelling provides a social context for literacy learning. By listening, children learn to attend to the messages and language of the storyteller and are exposed to a widening range of ideas and language. By providing children with opportunities to tell stories, we allow them to express their own experiences and learn about using language to communicate. Thus, storytelling allows children to begin to develop their thinking, their ideas, as they become invested in capturing and holding the attention of their listeners. This growing awareness of audience supports and prepares students for the more complex activities of academic reading and writing, where they will be developing more nuanced understanding of character and plot and theme. Storytelling leads to role taking and deepening understanding of inferences and understanding of literary themes. Finally, and most importantly for our bridges for families, storytelling taps into and celebrates children's prior knowledge.

CELEBRATING FAMILIES THROUGH STORYTELLING

Jessica, the teacher introduced in the opening story, seized upon her school's focus on thematic, integrated curriculum as a way to invite Rosina and her family to feel a greater part of the class and school, and in particular to celebrate Rosina's linguistic strength, her bilingualism. The topic for the spring was immigration. While the other third grade class was going to focus on Ellis Island and the period of immigration in the late nineteenth and early twentieth century, Jessica considered taking a different approach. What if, instead of starting with the past, she began her unit with the present as an opportunity to learn about the family stories of her class?

As she developed her family story project, she realized the importance of providing support for her students to share their stories and to value them within her classroom. It was important for all stories to be heard, not only the children who were confident and comfortable in speaking in front of a group. The project would provide the differentiation needed to include all children, even those struggling with literacy, to be an integral part of the unit. To do this she first developed an author study on the work of Patricia Polacco.

Author studies were the "required" curriculum plan at her school, but she was able to select and craft her own focus, as long as it met the standards.

They explored *Chicken Sunday* and *The Keeping Quilt* and began to use the books as mentor texts in narrative writing. Within these units, she stressed the importance of the details that made each story unique to the child and family. She then invited families to share their own traditions within the class and create family books together. The survey she developed is found in appendix 6.1.

Storytelling with Families

There are a variety of ways we can get to know students and their families' stories. Short sentence starters—for example, "I am happy when ...," "I worry about ..."—can be used with families as a way to initiate and spark a story. Instructional coach Peg Grafwallner (2017) believes it is essential for students to understand their family stories and presents three ideas to initiate the storytelling process. First, she suggests, ask students to interview a family member about a strong memory. Second, ask students to talk about who in their family they admire. She cautions to make sure that conceptions of family are inclusive. Finally, she argues that including classic children's stories and folktales are important experiences, whatever the age of children.

One powerful way to initiate family stories and bridge home and school is to invite children to share the history of their names. Naming traditions span cultures, and names are central to our identity. Unfortunately, too, names have become emblematic of inattention or dismissal of cultural relevance. Children's books such *My Name Is Sangoel* (Williams & Mohammed, 2009) recount how proud a young refugee, Sangoel, is about his name, but also the difficulties he experiences when his American teachers and schoolmates mispronounce it.

In *My Name Is Yoon* (Recrovits, 2014) a young Korean girl loves the way her name is written in Korean but struggles with its English equivalent. Other books that address these questions are *The Name Jar* by Choi (2003) and *Chrysanthemum* by Henkes (2008). Stories such as these highlight the multilayered meanings behind names and can be used to invite children to share the history and meaning of their names (see table 6.1 for other examples). In chapter 7 we discuss in greater depth the use of children's books to spark and connect conversations.

Another way to bring stories into the classroom and simultaneously build literacy skills, is by inviting children and families to participate in intergenerational literacy events. More formally, intergenerational literacy programs are designed to support literacy growth of children and adults. While there are many formalized and funded programs, such as Even Start,

Table 6.1. Children's Books about Names

My Name Is Sangoel (Williams & Mohammed, 2009)
My Name Is Yoon (Recorvits, 2014)
The Name Jar (Choi, 2003)
Chrysanthemum (Henkes, 2008)
Three Names of Me (Cummings, 2006)
Josephina Hates Her Name (Engel, 1999)
My Name Is Maria Isabel (Ada, 1995)
Hope (Monk, 1998)

whose goals are most directly focused on achievement, we are suggesting developing events and projects that unite students and family and community members in collaborative projects and activities. These can include interviewing community members to create oral histories.

Many existing social studies and ELA curricula have family and community as thematic elements or content. Others incorporate memoir as part of the reading and writing units. We urge extending the opportunities presented by these units to invite families into the conversation and to value the importance of telling and celebrating stories. It is also powerful, in particular for struggling readers, to use tangible objects to elicit stories. Bringing in old photographs can spark memories, stories, and rich conversations in ways a simple writing prompt cannot.

Similarly, a special object, one that means something to the family, can also be the catalyst for stories. As Winston (1997) shares, there are a variety of ways that family stories can be integrated into the curriculum. In particular, she urges teachers to consider finding opportunities within their curriculum to include spaces to acknowledge, explore, and celebrate strengths and stories that are part of families. These spaces should be flexible and adaptable to the unique contexts of the school and community. The Reading Rockets website provides excellent suggestions about how to incorporate family stories into the classroom (http://www.readingrockets. org/article/family-stories).

Within the classroom, teachers can preserve and share these curated stories. By creating books, both electronic and print, family stories become cherished texts for authentic reading. Rereading, for authentic purposes, is a key component in helping struggling readers develop fluency and comprehension. Because their stories come from and connect with home, they provide powerful motivation for shared readings at home and in school.

How to Become a Storyteller

(Adapted from Friday [2014])

1. Delve deeply into folktales, fairy tales, myths, and legends to discover the versions that you really like.
2. View professional storytellers so that you can understand different techniques.
3. Read to children using different voices.
4. Pick stories with a limited number of characters and repeating events to begin with as they are easier to remember.
5. Write the story down—writing helps us remember.
6. Create a "prop box" that you can use to help create the excitement of the story and use as tools for audience participation.

Sharing Stories through Food: Interdisciplinary Cooking Project

With rise in popularity of Food TV more and more children are aware of and enjoy cooking. While we may think that cooking is relegated to activities for very young children and preschoolers, food can become part of the curriculum and engage students and families in powerful ways. In particular, cooking is an interdisciplinary event and one that provides multiple access points for all kinds of learners.

Jenny, a fourth grade teacher, developed a project that integrated food and literacy, social studies, science, and math. Within this project, she introduced students to proverbs, short sayings that provide wisdom or advice, folktales and fairy tales in which food played a role, and nonfiction readings about baking and breads. The study of proverbs provided opportunities to explore metaphorical language in new ways.

Once students understood the meaning of proverbs, they interviewed family members about the proverbs they knew and brought in multilingual and multicultural examples of proverbs. The project culminated in a class cookbook that included contributions from all families, stories written by students after interviewing family members on the role the dish played in family tradition, and illustrations created by students and families.

As Jenny and her students were creating the book, several of the students grew so interested in the project that they asked if there could be cooking in school! When families, too, became excited, the project changed to involve families, when possible, cooking in school. For one student, this became an opportunity for his father, an accomplished home cook, to come into the classroom and shine. His dad commanded the attention of the students as he set out his tools, delegated tasks, and engaged the students in learning about the variety of Asian vegetables used in his stir-fry. As he cooked, he related the story of how he learned at the age of five in Vietnam, how to watch the rice pot and cut the vegetables, and then how he journeyed to the United States.

Interdisciplinary Cooking Project: Cross-Curricular Connections

Reading Connections
Students can develop reading skills from reading and writing recipes.

Writing Connections
Students can develop writing skills from reading and writing recipes.

Mathematics Connections
Students learn to double, halve, and so on different types of measurement systems.

Science Connections
Students learn about predicting what will happen and chemical reactions and experimentation with different times, different ingredients, and more as a way to integrate the scientific method.

Social Studies Connections
Foods come from different countries, different climates. Recipes are developed through different cultural practices and different histories. An overall unit on immigration can involve reading folktales, fairy tales, and food-related proverbs.

Create a Blog!

In 2010, Brandon Stanton, a New York City photographer, initiated a photography/storytelling project called Humans of New York. His initial goal was to photograph "10,000 New Yorkers on the street" and share, in their own words, something about them. This would be a kind of "catalogue" of the amazing diversity in the city. Through its popularity on social media, the project has grown to include best-selling books and recognition across the world. Readers respond to the immediacy of the photographs and stories Stanton shares. Cunningham (2015) notes that this genre, made recognizable through social media by Stanton, can serve as a tool for storytelling within classrooms and schools.

Morgan (2015) suggests teachers not only use blogs to enhance home–school communication (see chapters 3 and 4) but adds that class blogs create opportunities for students to share their ideas in a less formal genre and for authentic purposes. It helps position students in a collective and knowledgeable framework, especially important for struggling readers and writers. For example, Humans of Marshall Street Elementary School can become a collaborative effort between students, families, and educators to highlight the remarkable people who make up the school community. The blog can feature one or two people each week. Student-friendly platforms for blogs, which can be designated as public or private, include Kidblog, Glogster, Wonderopolis, Google Sites, MyStoryMaker, Tumblr, and Weebly.

In conclusion, it is essential to celebrate all the stories students and families bring to your classrooms. As Reese (2013) urges: "Family stories can be told nearly anywhere. They cost us only our time, our memories, our creativity.

They can inspire us, protect us, and bind us to others. So be generous with your stories and be generous in your stories. Remember that your children may have them for a lifetime."

SUMMARY

In this chapter, we explored the role storytelling plays in literacy development and the development of cultural identity. All families can provide students with opportunities for shared stories and discussion that promotes oral language development, a key component in reading. The inclusion and celebration of family stories in classroom activities supports the bridge between home and school.

Want to Know More?

- Visit the blogs and websites of storytellers to learn about their experiences and tips. Here are a few:
    http://lisawingate.com/blog3/storytelling-for-families/
    https://everpresent.com/family-storytelling-made-digital/
    http://www.colorincolorado.org/article/family-stories
- Experiment with a storytelling app such as StoryCatcher (http://storycatcherapp .com/).
- View videos of storytellers and storytelling approaches on YouTube to see the array of storytelling approaches. Some suggestions:
    https://www.youtube.com/user/Jbrary
    https://www.youtube.com/watch?v=rO3i_3WN7tk
    https://www.youtube.com/watch?v=JrZc6eztoH4
    https://www.youtube.com/watch?v=QEoEGr955tw
    https://www.youtube.com/watch?v=ylPhA3gTY84
- Read Keller & Franzak (2016), "When Names and Schools Collide: Critically Analyzing Depictions of Culturally and Linguistically Diverse Children Negotiating Their Names in Picture Books."

CHILDREN'S BOOKS

Polacco, P. (1992). *Chicken Sunday*. New York: Scholastic.
Polacco, P. (2000). *The keeping quilt.* New York: Scholastic.

APPENDIX 6.1 EXAMPLE OF A FAMILY TRADITIONS SURVEY

Dear Family,

Now that we have read some of Patricia Polacco's books and talked about how she remembers and writes about her family's traditions, we would like to include all students' traditions.

Please fill out this short survey to help us plan and understand all the kinds of traditions we have in our wonderful classroom community!

1. What is your favorite place to go as a family? What do you like about it?
2. What is your family's favorite meal? Who makes it best?
3. What is a special family day for you? What do you do on this day?

We would like to celebrate with you in class. What is one family tradition that you can share with us in school?

_____ I can bring to class _____

_____ I can bring a photo of _____

Thank you!

Chapter 7

Using Children's Literature to Connect Families and Schools

GUIDING PRINCIPLES IN ACTION THROUGH CHILDREN'S LITERATURE

Picture books can create a powerful stimulus for impactful dialogue. During a session of her children's literature class, Jenny, the instructor, read aloud *Last Stop on Market Street* (2015) by de la Peña. This book tells the story of a young boy, CJ, and his Nana as they take a bus ride on a Sunday afternoon. During the course of their journey, CJ expresses longing for what others have, such as a car or iPod, while Nana gently yet firmly points out the positive and beauty with each moment.

As Nana challenges CJ to see more deeply, the book itself challenges the reader to look more carefully and deeply at the story and his or her own preconceptions. One might expect that CJ and Nana are going to be clients at the soup kitchen they arrive at, yet in the final pages we learn that CJ and Nana are volunteers. This ending surprised the in-service teachers.

Teresa, a first-year first grade teacher exclaimed, "Wow—I wouldn't have expected that. I thought from the story that they were really poor." Samuel, a fourth grade teacher, countered, "But wait a minute, if you are poor you could also volunteer." The conversation grew deeper and deeper as the discussion, grounded in the book, challenged their own assumptions about poverty and urban environments. For example, Jenny and her students carefully considered a passage toward the end of the book in which CJ wondered about the dirty conditions of the street, while Nana explained the beauty she saw amidst the decay.

"Let's look at CJ's question," said Jenny. "Does that resonate for any of us? Is it something we wonder about as we walk in some areas where we teach?" By inviting her students to step into CJ's shoes and wonder, like CJ, about the reasons a neighborhood might have "crumbling sidewalks" and "boarded-up stores," Jenny uses the picture book as a way to push teachers to bring to the surface perspectives and possible biases, and to wrestle with them in a supportive context. As noted in earlier chapters, it is essential for teachers to recognize, name, and work toward shifting deficit views about certain communities, families, and children. Children's literature can play a pivotal role in this work.

Trust, collaborate, respect, adapt, and celebrate. These are key words outlining the five principles we articulate to guide teachers in building bridges of understanding with families of struggling readers. Through the previous chapters, we shared stories of families, teachers, and students; synthesized insights from relevant research; and provided practical suggestions to take into classrooms to foster bridge building.

In this chapter, we extend the conversation about bridging literacy learning for struggling readers, families, and schools by exploring how children's books are vital to all our principles. Children's literature provides the bridge between the enculturated literacy practices of the home and the literacy activities of the school. It provides a common language and broadens the understanding and knowledge of literacy and what we need to be successful. It reflects our cultural differences, our values as a community, our understandings or takes on life, and things we hold important to pass down to our children.

Who doesn't love a good story? Wells (1986) writes, "Storytelling is one of the most fundamental means whereby human beings gain control over the world around them ... storying is not a conscious and deliberate activity, but the way in which the mind itself works" (p. 197). Bishop (1990) describes the role of children's literature to serve as both mirror and window, a reflection of our own lives and experiences and a glimpse into the lives and experiences of others.

Both fiction and nonfiction contain stories we choose to pass on to children, powerful stories we, as teachers, parents, and grownups, hope will impact their lives. They can bridge any age and any interest when loved and shared. Hearne and Stephenson (2000) claim, "Old and young will smile in response to a funny picture, or concentrate on beautiful ones, or feel warm and secure with a cozy bedtime story, or sometimes get caught up in a tale of suspense" (p. 44). And as children move into chapter books, the characters become more complex, the conflicts become more complicated, the reader finds a place of his or her own. Whether one or one hundred, good books will be appealing, maybe not for the same reason, but something should grab each person interacting with the book.

Picture books are usually children's first introduction to literature. As the label indicates, the marriage of text and illustrations tell a story; dependent on one another, author and illustrator work together to complete the literary experience for reader and listener. A picture book is more than a sequence of words and illustrations. Rather, the most breathtaking art and the most memorable prose would remain lifeless on their own, compelling no page turns (Sutton & Parravano, 2010).

Children feel strongly, and their first reaction to a picture book will be visceral. The visual impact must be as important as the verbal impact (Hearne, 2000). "The finest picture books, after all, must appeal to the minds and hearts not only of the children to whom they are principally addressed but also of the grownups who select, buy, and read them aloud" (Spitz, 1999, p. 7). Spitz goes on to claim that picture books provide children with some of their earliest takes on morality, basic cultural knowledge, and messages about gender, race, and class. Al-Hazza (2010) states, "Stories, whether transmitted orally or through a written medium, are a powerful tool adults use to convey cultural values" (p. 63). They are meant to be shared and intended to be experiences with children. Picture books are museums on life.

"While books provide many opportunities for shared experience—reading aloud, discussion of books read in common, dramatization—books are best suited for one pair of hands at a time. That's how the story gets into the person, who can choose (or not) a multitude of ways to spread the word" (Sutton & Parravano, 2010, p. 113). Children moving into chapter books are independent readers with strong tastes and are ready, with willing adults and reading partners, to talk about the books they are reading across all genres. They are anxious to share what they learned, how they felt, what made them laugh or caused them to be curious or no longer feel alone.

In our work with struggling readers, we have found many children have not been exposed to high-quality literature, grownups excited about sharing picture books, or avenues of story into the world of literacy. Hearne (2000) states, "children don't learn how to read because they're supposed to but because they're surrounded by people who read and things that must be read. Literature is the road to literacy" (p. 213).

As Isaac Bashevis Singer (1978) stated in his Nobel Prize lecture, "There is no paradise for bored readers and no excuse for tedious literature that does not intrigue the reader, uplift him, give him the joy and the escape that true art always grants."

MATCHING TEXTS WITH STRUGGLING READERS

There is a book for everyone, on every topic, in every genre, for every reader. It all boils down to finding the right book for the right child. As teachers, parents, and grownups, we become the liaisons between the thousands of children's books out there and the children we know. For struggling readers, the opportunity to engage with authentic texts becomes limited, as teachers too often rely on commercially prepared materials rather than explore instructional and motivational potentials of a wider range of texts (Allington, 2011; Dreher, 2003; Worthy, 1996).

Rhodes and Dudley-Marling (1998) remind us that development in reading can only take place in an environment where children frequently read for meaning. Most effective teachers were able to match struggling readers with lots of books that matched their interests and reading levels. In a study conducted by Tuten and Jensen (2009), teachers working with struggling readers in a clinical experience selected books to engage readers, texts that were relatable, entertaining, and graphically appealing, matched to children's current reading abilities. This, in turn, allowed the children to build confidence as readers. In their book selection for struggling readers, the teachers selected books that challenged children, introduced a new genre, gave an important message, or developed background knowledge.

Self-Reflection Activity

Donalyn Miller (2009) suggests teachers participate in a self-reflection activity to learn about themselves as readers. We offer those questions here in order for you to consider how your view of reading is reflected in your instruction, literacy activities, and book selection:

- What were your reading experiences as a child?
- Were these positive or negative experiences for you?
- Do you see yourself as a reader?
- How do you share your reading experiences—both current and those from the past—with your students and their parents?
- With which group of readers in your classroom do you most identify?
- Who have been your reading role models?
- List five books you have read.
- How long did it take you to read them?
- Which books were read for a job- or school-related purpose?
- Which books were read for pleasure? (Miller, 2009, p. 111)

The use of children's literature can build on our five principles. Each of those principles, in relationship to children's literature, are discussed below. We offer a list of children's books in appendix 7.1 related to each principle.

The list is some of our favorites, ones we go to time and time again. However, this is in no way a complete list of books we have found useful in the many classrooms in which we have worked. We have listed websites to use for finding books that will work for you and for your students and their families. You know them best.

USING CHILDREN'S LITERATURE TO BUILD TRUST

Dana and Lynch-Brown (1993; cited in Escamilla & Nathenson-Mejía, 2003) delineate four reasons why it is important for teacher candidates to read and discuss diverse children's literature.

- Vicarious access to a wider world of experiences
- Appreciation and understanding of cultural experiences
- Insights into children's feelings and thoughts
- Knowledge of a greater range of books to use as a teacher

We would extend this importance to in-service teachers, much like the example that begins this chapter. Teachers at all stages of their careers benefit from opportunities to deepen their background knowledge and ability to make connections with children and families as they read more and more diverse books. Escamilla and Nathenson-Mejía (2003) engaged preservice teachers in extensive reading and discussion of Latino/a-focused children's books while those teachers were in student teaching placements in primarily Spanish-speaking schools.

The readings and focused discussions served to increase the teacher candidates' background knowledge and helped them make connections with their students. The authors found the project helped preservice teachers connect on a human level, based on how we are all alike, denying the unique perspectives different cultures bring to a situation. They discovered that more direct conversations were needed for preservice teachers to recognize or value differences.

Teachers and preservice teachers need opportunities to explore strengths found in every family, facing common or extreme struggles. "Children live in a world of diverse opportunities for learning, in which literacy is an important vehicle for this to occur" (Cairney, 2002, p. 153). Teachers need to understand the differences between literacy at home and at school as a starting point on which to build relationships of trust.

In her literacy methods course with preservice teachers, Charlene uncovered the importance of gathering African American children's books focused on family strengths to share during an annual African American Read In held each February. Her preservice teachers came to understand the power of sharing stories with relatable characters from diverse home cultures. One preservice teacher discovered, "The children were so amazed to see themselves, and their family, in the book we shared. One girl shouted out during the reading, 'Her grandma looks like my grandma!' You could see the excitement on the children's faces when we were sharing the story."

Appendix 7.1 at the end of the chapter presents titles that can expand teachers' understandings of the rich diversity of families and the many strengths families bring to the challenges they face. These books can serve as catalysts, such as in the opening example, to deepen discussions and insights and lead to empathetic, authentic bridges between home and school.

Parent Connection

During a family literacy gathering at Clariton School when parents discussed potential family–child book conversations evolving from *Whoever You Are* (Fox, 1997), a mom relayed this recent discussion with her son.
My son is biracial (white and Puerto Rican). The other day my son decided to draw a picture of himself when he is one hundred years old and he had a dark brown face. He explained, "I will be black when I am one hundred." I tried to explain how you stay the same color. At our school, these kids do not see racial difference as a problem.

USING CHILDREN'S LITERATURE TO COLLABORATE WITH FAMILIES

When teachers ask families to read with their children at home, many go home confused or unsure of what that means and what they should be doing. For families of struggling readers, what practices they should be employing at home are even fuzzier, often resulting in trying to duplicate strategies used in the classroom. In chapter 3 we discussed the importance of ensuring that home and school communication is built on trust and genuine collaboration.

One of the teacher's important tasks is to help parents understand how children become readers (Enz, 1995) and the role they can play in assisting them to become successful. Parents need clearly defined roles the teacher expects them to play. Parents might want support and suggestions for interacting with their child at home. However, it is important not to predetermine the kinds of roles parents can play. As seen in earlier chapters, families bring a wealth of experiences to supporting their children and may bristle when viewed, by teachers, in a limited way. When parents have access to the literacy practices and literacy-related activities and materials teachers use with struggling readers, children's progress is enhanced (McCarthey, 2000). Epstein (2001) found more involved parents had been given directions and specific suggestions for supporting their children's literacy development at home.

Students' independent reading with their families can be centered around a central theme being studied in the classroom. Books consistent with each student's literacy strengths, across genres, can be chosen for family reading. If, for example, your current social studies theme is Holocaust studies, a variety of books can be made available to students. Consider how rich the conversations will be about the Holocaust when so many varying perspectives and different sources of information are shared. All students, regardless of their different reading strengths and vulnerabilities, can actively participate by having something genuine to offer from their independent reading with their families.

Parent Book Clubs to Build Collaboration

Although the teacher needs to know the literacy activities of the home, it is also important for the parent to be informed of the literacy events at school. Larrotta and Gainer (2008) found parents, no matter their level of formal education, were highly motivated to read with their children and to engage with related assignments and even requested more readings to share with their children. A list of possible books related to school assignments can be found in appendix 7.2.

"What did you do in school today?" "What are you reading in school?" "Did you complete your twenty minutes of reading tonight?" Questions we all ask our children. They are empty questions designed to show an interest or to monitor children's responsibilities. They are not the questions we need to ask to extend the rich conversations we want to have with children about what they are reading. We want them to have conversations similar to those Jenny's students had around *Last Stop on Market Street*. This may be foreign to some families who may be familiar with the narrow literacy instruction focusing on literal comprehension used with many struggling readers and unfamiliar with readers bringing meaning to the text from their prior knowledge and experiences. How to get to those conversations can remain a mystery.

Inviting families to participate in book clubs using the same books children will be reading in and for school gives them the experience so they understand the concept. For example, if the class is going to be reading *Bridge to Terabithia* by Katherine Paterson, the family book club would read the book before the class embarks on it. Books with dramatic plot structures have the greatest power to propel us into the world of story. Interest in the book is so important in the construction of meaning, and families have the interest because these are the books their children are reading.

As in most book clubs, participants read the book in advance of the book club. They come together for talk about what they have read. In a parent book club with fifth grade parents run by Deborah, conversations around the books deepened parents' understanding of ideas in the text. She found that parents owned their book club and their reactions to the books, not necessarily what they thought their children would think or how their children would react.

Parents were also questioning the authors, negotiating meaning with other book club members, and making text-to-self connections. They would stop in the street and in the supermarket to discuss the books they were reading in book club, asking what part they were up to and what they were thinking so far. In book club one night, a mom said, "I really found that even when we met, we'd stop on the street or see each other, did you read it? Did you get to that part yet? No, I didn't. All right, I won't tell you."

Graduate student Anne, working with Charlene, offered busy families another way to stay involved in their child's independent reading at home through family message journals (see the Worlds of Words website, https://wowlit.org/go/wow-currents/page/36/). Anne's study of family vacations enabled a small group of reluctant readers to conduct written conversations with family members using children's books like *Isabel's House of Butterflies*. One third grader discovered his mother's knowledge of Spanish when he simply asked, "Do you know any Spanish words?" to close his journal entry. Their extended written conversation allowed Anne to build on this interest in bilingual and nonfiction texts in further home–school book explorations.

Having had the experience, families can replicate the conversations from book club at home, and conversations about their school reading are enhanced and personalized. They know their children and can personalize the discussions. One parent, when discussing the book club, stated, "Yeah, we did so much more as a parent group than they did in class. I think that's why I was a little disappointed in the class discussions, which may be normal for a fifth grade discussion." Without having the parent book club experience, the parent and child would not have had the opportunity to delve deeper into the book than the teacher alone would have done with the class. (See appendix 7.3 for a sample letter to parents.)

USING CHILDREN'S LITERATURE TO BUILD RESPECT

In a recent *PBS NewsHour* article, novelist Jesmyn Ward said, "When you see yourself reflected in literature ... it enlarges your ideas of what is possible for you." According to the Cooperative Children's Book Center at the University of Wisconsin, in 2016, 22 percent of children's books were written or illustrated by, or written about, people of color. We are each different from one another, but it is the common bonds that allow us to celebrate our differences and similarities. When we discover how we are linked together, we find mutual respect. In chapter 4, we discussed the importance of building respect through capturing home literacy experiences. Respect is extended in our discussion of children's books.

Beaty (1997) states that to develop respect what counts most is the following:

- A deep *belief* in the worth of every child
- An accepting *attitude* toward each child as a unique individual
- Unqualified *support* for each child's development of emotional, social, physical, cognitive, language, and creative skills on a daily basis (p. 4)

We extend this to the families of struggling readers, where belief, attitude, and support have not always been respected. When we build a system of trust by using diverse and culturally relevant children's books with families of struggling readers, we build respect for each other and find the bonds we share. The similarities that bring us together, and the different talents, skills, and abilities we bring to the world, need to be present in our work.

Continually Expanding Knowledge of Diverse Books

In their book *More Mirrors in the Classroom: Using Urban Children's Literature to Increase Literacy*, Fleming, Catapano, Thompson, and Carrillo (2016) argue that it is critical for all children to be immersed in books that authentically represent their cultural and linguistic identities. They suggest ten key steps for teachers to begin to make this happen:

1. Extend and supplement current classroom book collections.
2. Explore ever-growing websites and publishers for high-quality children's literature.
3. Ensure a single book does not represent a culture: "strength in numbers."
4. Invite readers to participate in text selection and review.
5. Act when more books are needed.
6. Integrate diverse books within the established curriculum.
7. Create critical literacy inquiries and units to support literacy as a means for social justice.
8. Embrace books with strong themes.
9. Discover your own advocacy role.
10. Enjoy the exploration.

As discussed in chapter 4, literacy bridges are formed and strengthened when teachers actively reach out to understand their students' and their families' lives outside classroom walls. Incorporating books that authentically represent those experiences builds trust. For example, books such as *I Read Signs* by Tana Hoban or *City Signs* by Zoran Milich demonstrate the value of environmental print and the literacies experienced in everyday life. Books show families how you respect their literate ways of knowing different from school.

We recommend these online children's literature websites focused on sharing diverse life experiences:

- Worlds of Words children's and young adult literature website (www .wowlit.org)
- American Library Association children's and young adult book awards, such as the Coretta Scott King Award for African American books (http:// www.ala.org/awardsgrants/coretta-scott-king-book-awards) and the Pura Belpré Award for Latino books (http://www.ala.org/alsc/awardsgrants/ bookmedia/belpremedal/belprepast)
- We Need Diverse Books (http://www.diversebooks.org/ourstory/)
- And from NCTE, read a blog post with links to prominent authors (http:// www2.ncte.org/blog/2017/09/students-right-need-read-diverse-books/)

Embracing and seeking out diverse children's literature is particularly important in providing engaging, inviting access points to readers who may not believe that reading is "for them." Putting the right book in the hands of a reader at the right time is critical.

One mirror to highlight here is that of learners who struggle. As well as providing children with books in which they can identify culturally with characters, it's important for children, especially those who experience struggles with learning, struggle to find their place socially, or whose family and life experiences are marginalized, to find characters and plots that resonate. Sharing these books with families supports deeper understanding.

In addition to validating these complex feelings and experiences, books should provide opportunities to experience the joys of reading where new insights into literacy learning are a by-product of the experience. A list of books we particularly enjoy can be found in appendix 7.4.

3, 2, 1 STOP AND THINK

---

3. Identify three children's books you use in your classroom to address cultural diversity.

2. Identify two things you have learned that are unique to one of those cultures.

1. Create one plan to celebrate the differences you have found between cultures.

USING CHILDREN'S LITERATURE TO ADAPT THE CURRICULUM

In an insightful study, Robertson and Reese (2017) investigated which genres parents read to children and which they read for themselves. While parents reported reading more narrative picture books to their children, they enjoyed reading expository books themselves. They suggest, "sharing a wide range of genres is important because it may foster parent-child book sharing. Each genre may bring somewhat different benefits for children's language and literacy development" (p. 18).

The main goal, according to Hornsby (2000), of a take-home reading program is for children to share positive reading experiences with people who are significant to their lives. As you recall from chapter 5, it is important for families to be able to successfully support home literacy activities, whether these are traditional homework or extension activities.

Teacher Connection

Lauren supports family adaptation through the use of take-home book bags:

Many of my parents are working professionals and are able to take time off to come into school at the beginning or end of a school day to take part in an activity, but for others it is hard to do that. So, taking into account the lifestyles and availability of all of my parents, I decided to plan a combination of in-school visits with a book baggie and logbook for students to take home and work on with their parents. I chose to add on the book baggie because I have received questions from parents about how to best support their child with reading and questions about the science topics studied at school.

Parents in my class are always asking me about the "right way" to approach aiding a child in reading at home and checking for comprehension. I decided to address this question by providing a lesson where they can come into class and watch me model a read-aloud using growth and mindset/accountable-talk questions and answer stems.

I have a very culturally diverse class, with Spanish and Korean being spoken at home. I was able to translate the parent letter, question stems, and book baggie directions into both languages with the help of colleagues in my building. I also have the ability to ask my bilingual colleagues to make themselves available for parent visits to be able to translate anything that is going on in the classroom for the model lesson or the end-of-the-unit celebration.

According to Puzio and her colleagues (2017), a common misconception teachers have is that the classroom must match or duplicate the students' home environments. Family members know their children's strengths and interests, the perfect spot to start for positive interactions with books and increased motivation for reading. They see their children in various settings, using reading in different ways from school (see chapter 4).

In adapting books to support the curriculum, families should be offered a variety of books from which to choose. Children are more highly motivated to read books of their own choosing (Loera, Rueda, & Nakamoto, 2011). It also helps develop a sense of ownership of their own literacy learning (Herold, 2011) (see appendix 7.5).

Teacher Connection

Lara shares the importance of helping children find their reading identity:

I had a student come in this year. He's in fifth grade and he told me he didn't have a favorite book. And I thought that was a big deal because even if it's a picture book, even if it's Green Eggs and Ham *or whatever it is, it's a big deal. And I took that very personally, as a challenge, and it turns out that it wasn't that much of a challenge because he's loved everything that he's reading, so I'm going to tell you the way I developed that with him and the way I kept his mother in the loop about that. Conferencing, I have learned over the years, is the number one way to know my readers and to push my readers from level to level. Some of my students need me to meet with them two times a week, some once a week, some twice a month, some once a month.*

Using Children's Literature to Celebrate Families

In chapter 6 we highlighted the important ways family stories can serve as a foundation to an asset-based and inclusive perspective on literacy development and family engagement. By validating and celebrating families' personal and cultural stories, particularly through oral storytelling, struggling readers have rich, authentic, affirming opportunities to increase their literacy skills.

There is also a wealth of children's books that capture the wide range of traditional folktales and modern family stories that resonate with children and families, and many of these kinds of text are probably already in your classroom, school, or local library. Yet, as important as it is to bring multicultural texts into classrooms, it is equally important to carefully evaluate and consider the authenticity of texts and consider if some may contain inaccuracies or, worse, perpetuate stereotypes.

Children's book author and illustrator Grace Lin (2012) provides a detailed analysis of the inaccuracies of a favorite book, *Tikki Tikki Tembo* by Arlene Mosel, to argue for just such a kind of reading. Short, Day, and Schroeder (2016), in their book *Teaching Globally*, share a wealth of resources to support explorations of different cultures through accurate, authentic, and meaningful children's books. Textboxes 7.1 and 7.2 provide web-based resources for engaging in a critical review of texts.

Textbox 7.1 Resources to Explore Folktales

- "Hispanic Heritage," http://www.colorincolorado.org/booklist/folk-tales-and -legends-hispanic-heritage
- "Bengali Folktales and Fairy-Tales," https://naztanu.wordpress.com/2017/08/07/ bengali-folktales-and-fairy-tales/
- "10 African and African American Folktales for Children," https://www.nypl .org/blog/2017/02/01/10-african-and-african-american-folktales-celebrate-black -history-month
- "Native American Indian Legends and Folklore," http://www.native-languages.org/ legends.htm
- "Children's Author Shares Her Armenian Culture through Stories," https:// kidworldcitizen.org/childrens-author-shares-armenian-culture-stories/
- "We Need Diverse Books," https://diversebooks.org/
- "Where Can I Find Diverse Children's Books," http://blog.leeandlow.com/2014/03/21/ where-can-i-find-great-diverse-childrens-books/

Textbox 7.2 Blogs That Recommend Diverse Books (adapted from Lee and Low Publishers)

African American books	https://thebrownbookshelf.com/
	https://grassrootscommunityfoundation .org/1000-black-girl-books-resource-guide/
Native American books	https://americanindiansinchildrensliterature .blogspot.com/
Latino/a books	https://latinosinkidlit.com/
Asian books and perspective	http://www.gracelin.com/
Diverse young adult books	http://richincolor.com/
LBGTQ books for young readers	http://www.leewind.org/
Diverse books for young readers	https://campbele.wordpress.com/
Diverse books and lists, many bilingual Spanish/English	http://www.colorincolorado.org/
Lee and Low books on Pinterest—all areas	https://www.pinterest.com/leeandlow/

Throughout a school year, teachers can draw on family resources to celebrate family cultural and social traditions. See appendix 7.6 for some of our favorite texts that support this celebration. For example, you can create an African American read-in to show families how you value their culture through reading. In coordination with peers, families and children move through classrooms of teachers or preservice teachers who share award-winning African American authors. Similarly, there can be an evening for

Dia de los Ninos to celebrate Latino children's books. This can be facilitated with any culture and demonstrates respect for families' cultures and funds of knowledge. In chapter 8, we discuss further how a school can embrace the structure of community reads to celebrate literacy and community beyond individual teachers' classrooms.

DEVELOPING WORKSHOPS FOR FAMILY EDUCATION

Teachers should not assume family members know how to help their struggling readers. In fact, Paratore and Jordan (2007) believe that "helping parents to understand why particular practices are important to children is an important first step in encouraging parents to add recommended activities and interactions to their family routines" (p. 696).

Family members may not be skilled readers themselves. Many interpret that their child is not bright and are concerned they have done something wrong to cause the problem the child has with literacy acquisition. Their own inability to read and write causes them to be frightened and dismayed by their child's inability to adequately read in school (Lipson & Wixson, 2003). Teachers need to listen to family members' concerns, questions, and frustrations when trying to help their struggling readers at home. "Also, an effective teacher communicates to parents about ways to engage their child in authentic literacy tasks at home, where reading for meaning is emphasized" (Herold, 2011, p. 40). Loera, Rueda, and Nakamoto (2011) found most Latino families are not aware of the full range of literacy resources that exist in school, and when they do become aware of them, they do not know how to access them.

Teachers can inform family members about various materials and books (as discussed above) that are likely to capture the interest of their children struggling with literacy acquisition (Baker, 2003). A study of Latino families by Loera, Rueda, and Nakamoto (2011) suggests parents' understanding of their active role in promoting reading practices at home is an important factor and an effective strategy to increase children's engagement in literacy learning.

Baker (2003) claims, "Shared storybook reading plays an important role in providing reading motivation. When the affective climate is positive, children are more interested in reading and more likely to view it as enjoyable" (p. 101). Collaboration between home and school is necessary to capture the interest and motivation of struggling readers.

Larrotta and Gainer (2008) designed an after-school literacy project for immigrant parents to help them learn about the educational system in the United States, with a focus on literacy-related issues. The parents participated in hands-on learning, engaging in the reading process using culturally relevant children's books. The project had two goals: to teach comprehension strategies, and to have parents teach comprehension strategies to their children. This would be especially important for parents who were not only confused about the educational system itself but also by the issues around literacy acquisition for struggling readers.

For children struggling with literacy, help from family members is crucial to their ongoing achievement. As DeFauw and Burton (2009) report, parents need to be supportive and give encouragement to guide their children's literacy development and understand how that translates to successful practices at home. They designed training programs at the University of Michigan for parents of children attending their reading clinic. Their series of workshops focused on fluency, comprehension, explanation of various genres, models of read-alouds, varied strategies for word study to develop stronger vocabularies, and other topics. Similarly, Herold (2011) conducted a series of workshops for parents of struggling readers throughout the school year.

When working with families of struggling readers, family literacy gatherings provide a venue where both parents and teachers share their literacy knowledge (Endrizzi, 2008). Children's literature becomes the vehicle for families, children, and their teachers to talk about and demonstrate what they know about literacy, to cross literacy bridges. Children's books, as Miller (2009) reminds us, become experiences when opened and shared. See appendix 7.7 for texts about reading and literacy.

SUMMARY

In this chapter, we discussed how children's books help develop the five guiding principles as a literacy bridge between families and schools. It is important to consider the interests of families and struggling readers when selecting and recommending children's literature. Families are often confused about how best to share books with their children, and carefully designed workshops with clear instructions, expectations, and practice sessions are beneficial. We encourage you to explore ways to assist families. Various websites, lists of our favorite books, and texts to access additional information are contained in this chapter.

Want to Know More?

The following books help you discover and share with families the joy of reading:

- Fox's (2008) *Reading Magic: Why Reading Aloud to Our Children Will Change Their Lives Forever.*
- Miller's (2009) *The Book Whisperer: Awakening the Inner Reader in Every Child.*
- Sutton and Parravano's (2010) *A Family of Readers: The Book Lover's Guide to Children's and Young Adult Literature.*

Explore and share with families these digital libraries:

- https://www.getepic.com/, a digital library that includes audio books and bilingual books
- http://www.uniteforliteracy.com/, digital books in many languages, primarily for younger readers

Learn more about using new technologies to support reading growth:

- Cahill, M., & McGill-Franzen, A. (2013). Selecting "app" ealing and "app" ropriate book apps for beginning readers. *Reading Teacher, 67*(1), 30–39.

CHILDREN'S BOOKS

de la Peña, M. (2015). *Last stop on Market Street*. New York: G. P. Putnam's Sons.

Hoban, T. (1987). *I read signs*. New York: Greenwillow Books.

Milich, Z. (2005). *City signs*. Toronto: Kids Can Press.

Mosel, A. (1968). *Tikki tikki tembo*. New York: Henry Holt & Co.

Paterson, K. (1977). *Bridge to Terabithia*. New York: HarperCollins.

Ringgold, F. (1991). *Tar beach*. New York: Scholastic.

APPENDIX 7.1

Appendix 7.1 Stories for Trust

Title and Author	Format	Synopsis
The Keeping Quilt by Patricia Polacco	Picture book	Russian Jewish immigrants use old clothes to make a quilt that serves different purposes through four generations.
The Quiet Place by Sarah Stewart	Picture book	A story of immigration and assimilation set in the 1950s. The story is told through Isabel's letters to her Aunt Lupita in Mexico.
Two White Rabbits by Jairo Buitrago	Wordless picture book	An immigrant father and daughter complete a complex journey north from Mexico.
A Shelter in Our Car by Monica Gunning	Picture book	A homeless mother and son cope while living in a car.
Maddi's Fridge by Lois Brandt	Picture book	A young girl helps a friend deal with food insecurity in a sensitive manner.
Chocolate Me by Taye Diggs	Picture book	A young boy discovers the beauty of his different skin and hair to overcome bullies.
Stepping Stones by Magriet Ruurs	Picture book	A migrant family flees their Muslim country for safety.
Tree of Cranes by Allen Say	Picture book	Set in Japan, the story of a boy's first Christmas. Illustrations allow for conversation about Japanese culture—tatami mats, kimonos, origami, etc.
Who's in a Family by Robert Skutch	Picture book	A nonfiction book that presents a range of family structures for children to see themselves and classmates within.
Wonder by R. J. Palacio	Chapter book	A moving, funny, and ultimately transformative story of a talented child with a facial abnormality who enters school at fifth grade. Highlights the unique strengths of family and school staff.
Ghost by Jason Reynolds	Chapter book	First in a series, the first-person story of a young man's challenges as he wrestles with a difficult family history, school demands, and his desire to excel at track.

APPENDIX 7.2

Appendix 7.2 Stories for Collaboration

Title and Author	Format	Synopsis	Curriculum Connection
Sugar by Jewell Parker Rhodes	Chapter book	Set in Louisiana on a plantation in 1870, ten-year-old Sugar works the fields. We learn of her friendship with Billy, the son of the former master, and the arrival of laborers from China.	Social studies: Reconstruction
All the Water in the World by George Ella Lyon and Katherine Tillotson	Picture book	A book written in rhyme with gorgeous illustrations sharing facts about water and water conservation.	Science: Water cycle
A Cool Drink of Water by Barbara Kerley	Picture book	A photo book filled with rich images of people using water resources wisely.	Science: Water conservation
Isabel's House of Butterflies by Tony Johnston	Picture book	A girl's family struggles to decide whether to save their trees for the monarch butterflies' annual migration or cut down the trees to sell.	Science: Butterfly migration and tree conservation
Curious Garden by Peter Brown	Picture book	On an abandoned set of tracks in New York City, a boy tends the few growing plants and then adds to the garden. Inspired by Highline Park.	Science: Planting
In the Garden: Who's Been Here? by Lindsey Barrett George	Picture book	Children are invited to explore the birds, insects, and animals commonly found in gardens.	Science: Gardening
Dumpster Diver by Janet Wong	Picture book	Steve, an electrician, dumpster dives with children from his apartment building. The objects they find are turned into useful things.	Science: Recycling
Math Curse by Jon Scieszka	Picture book	A girl's math teacher says there is math in everything, and as the day goes on she finds math in everything and believes it is a curse.	Math: Concepts in everyday living

Place Where Sunflowers Grow by Amy Lee-Tai	Picture book	Inspired by her family's story, Mari wonders how anything could bloom in the desert of their internment camp.	Social studies: Japanese internment camps
A Is for Activist by Innosanto Nagara	Picture book for older readers	Adolescents will be inspired to explore social justice issues.	Social studies: Workers and activists
Malala, a Brave Girl from Pakistan/ Iqbal, a Brave Boy from Pakistan by Jeannette Winter	Picture book	Two heroic teens fight for equal rights and social justice.	Social studies: Educational inequality

APPENDIX 7.3

Appendix 7.3 Camille's Invitation for Family Book Club

Dear Families,

We are so excited to announce that we are now starting a book club. This book club involves YOU dear families! We have chosen seven of our favorite books that we hope you and your daughter will enjoy.

Every month, beginning in October, we will read a new book! This will continue until May, but due to winter break we will not have a book in December. On the first of the month, look out for your first book letter in your daughter's folder! The letter will include the book title, the chapters we would like you to read that week, questions to ask your daughter to ensure understanding, and some discussion topics so your family can really dive into this text!

At the end of every month, we will have our official book club meeting! Look out for more information on when/where we will meet in each book letter. There will be coffee and pastries served while we discuss our favorite (and least favorite) parts of the book.

We hope to have every family involved for each book, but we understand that life can get in the way. Try to keep up as best you can, and if you miss out one month, no big deal! Join us for the next book!

Month	Title	Author	Why we read it
October	*Judy Moody Declares Independence*	Megan McDonald	Judy just wants to express herself. It is important that girls/women always find ways to express themselves! This book also directly connects to our core value, responsibility.
November	*Sugar Plum Ballerinas*	Whoopi Goldberg	This is about a girl who moves to Harlem and has to find herself. Girls can begin to empathize with new students in their class.
January	*Call Me Maria*	Judith Ortiz Cofer	This is a story of a young girl's journey as she tries to assimilate in her new home in New York after leaving her home in Puerto Rico. The girls often empathize with Maria, and it gives them understanding of the trials and tribulations she goes through.
February	*The Miniature World of Marvin and James*	Elise Broach	This book gives the girls practice with understanding perspectives in a fun and cool way. This one is always a hit!

March	*Toys Go Out*	Emily Jenkins	This story is about bravery and forgiveness. At this point in the school year, girls are often having friendship issues with one another. Forgiveness is important for us to think about at this time.
April	*Like Pickle Juice on a Cookie*	Julie Sternberg	There is a strong lesson a little girl has to learn in this book. Our girls can relate big time to this story!
May	*The Miraculous Journey of Edward Tulane*	Kate DiCamillo	Edward goes on a miraculous journey and finds himself. The girls will go on their own journey throughout second grade (by the time they read this, the journey will almost be over)!

Looking forward to sharing the books with you! Please let me know if you have questions!

Sincerely,
Ms Camille

APPENDIX 7.4

Appendix 7.4 Stories for Respect

Title and Author	Format	Synopsis
Ninth Ward by Jewel Parker Rhodes	Chapter book	In New Orleans, twelve-year-old Lanesta lives with her caregiver, Mama Ya-Ya, who speaks to the spiritual world and predicts the devastation of Hurricane Katrina. Lanesta must navigate personal and physical challenges.
The Hate U Give by Angie Thomas	Chapter book	Starr struggles to face the death of her best friend in a police shooting
Shooting Kabul by N. H. Senzai	Chapter book	Chronicles a Muslim family's horrific flight from Afghanistan to America and their efforts to find a lost child.
Amazing Grace by Mary Hoffman	Picture book	Grace loves stories and reenacts them. When she wants to play Peter Pan in the upcoming school play, she must overcome stereotypes.
Separate Is Never Equal by Duncan Tonatiuh	Picture book	Sylvia Mendez's family fought to offer her an equal education ten years before Ruby Bridges faced desegregation.
Knock Knock: My Dad's Dream for Me by Daniel Beaty	Picture book	A son comes to understand how much his father loves him in spite of his absence from his daily life.
Taking Sides by Gary Soto	Chapter book	Lincoln moves to a new school where he experiences challenges as a Latino. This book addresses the role of sports as a component in schooling experiences.
Those Shoes by Maribeth Boelts	Picture book	Jeremy wants the sneakers everyone seems to be wearing at school. His grandmother tells him he needs boots for winter and they do not have room for "want."
I Am Not Your Perfect Mexican Daughter by Erica Sanchez	Chapter book	A coming-of-age story that realistically relates the generational and cultural tensions of a young woman navigating family and future.

APPENDIX 7.5

Appendix 7.5 Stories for Adaptation

Title and Author	Format	Synopsis	Curriculum Connection
Esperanza Rising by Pam Munoz Ryan	Chapter book	After her father dies, Esperanza and her family must leave Mexico. They flee to California and must work as laborers.	Social studies: Great Depression, immigration, migrant workers
Inside Out & Back Again by Thanhha Lai	Chapter book	Autobiographical. Her experiences as a refugee fleeing Vietnam.	Social studies: Vietnam, refugees
One Crazy Summer by Rita Williams-Garcia	Chapter book	Three sisters are sent to Oakland, California, by their father to live with their mother who had abandoned them. It is 1968, and the girls attend a Black Panther camp.	Social studies: Family dynamics, social services, and radical groups
Out of the Dust by Karen Hesse	Chapter book	Written in free verse, historical fiction about the Great Depression set in Oklahoma.	Social studies: Dust Bowl.
Train to Somewhere by Eve Bunting	Picture book	A girl is sure her mother will be at one of the train stops as she travels west with other orphans.	Social studies: Orphan Train Movement, 1850–1920

APPENDIX 7.6

Appendix 7.6 Stories for Celebration

Title and Author	Format	Synopsis
Beautiful Blackbird by Ashley Bryan	Picture book	A folktale from Zambia that explains how birds get their black markings.
The Roots of My Family Tree by Niki Alling	Picture book	A little girl takes a trip around the world to celebrate and learn about the different facets of her cultural background.
Saturday Sancocho by Leyla Torres	Picture book	Maria Lili enjoys making sancocho with her grandparents each Saturday. She ends up at the market for ingredients.
A Different Pond by Bao Phi	Picture book	A young Vietnamese boy, Bao, and his father fish together before his father goes off to work. Develops an understanding of their relationship as new immigrants.
Tar Beach by Faith Ringgold	Picture book	A story told through the images of a quilt, part memory, part fantasy, integrating family history from New York City during the Great Depression.
Thunder Cake by Patricia Polacco	Picture book	A grandmother and child use a family recipe to make a special cake during a thunderstorm.
Wilfred Gordon McDonald Partridge by Mem Fox	Picture book	A little boy lives next to a nursing home and befriends the people who live there.
Junebug by Alice Mead	Chapter book	First in a series for younger readers about a young African American boy navigating his own dreams and the challenges of his neighborhood.
Does My Head Look Big in This? by Randa Abdel-Fattah	Chapter book	Teenager Amal chooses to wear the hijab, and this book follows her through experiences with friends, classmates, and family in both a humorous and insightful way.

APPENDIX 7.7

Appendix 7.7 Stories for Insights into Literacy

Title and Author	Format	Synopsis
The Best Book to Read by Debbie Bertram and Susan Boom	Picture book	A librarian shares the wide range of books available in the library.
How to Teach a Slug to Read by Susan Pearson	Picture book	A boy explains the reading rules mama slug uses to teach her baby slug to read. They include be patient and read aloud.
I Will Not Read This Book by Cece Meng	Picture book	Humorous story of a boy who claims he won't read the book in a series of silly situations.
The Library by Sarah Stewart	Picture book	Elizabeth Brown loves books more than dolls and toys. She has so many they are hard to fit in her room.
Dear Juno by Soyung Pak	Picture book	Juno in America and his grandmother in Korea are pen pals, but neither speaks the other's language. It illustrates alternative ways of communication.
Tomas and the Library Lady by Pat Mora	Picture book	Tomas and his family are migrant workers. His family has a rich storytelling tradition that is enhanced when Tomas enters the library and discovers the world of books.
Thank you, Mr. Falker by Patricia Polacco	Picture book	An autobiographical story of Trisha's struggles with learning to read and the teacher who helps unlock literacy with her.
My Name Is Brain/Brian by Jeanne Betancourt	Chapter book	Story of a sixth grade boy whose unidentified and supported reading issues cause him to feel isolated. When he receives help, his confidence and self-esteem increase.
Eleven by Patricia Reilly Giff	Chapter book	An engaging and suspenseful mystery as well as a moving story of a young man with learning challenges seeking to better understand himself and his family.
Hank Zipzer: Niagara Falls or Does It? By Henry Winkler	Chapter book	First of a series featuring Hank Zipzer, a fourth grade boy whose creativity isn't always applauded in the classroom. Humorous and relatable to children who may be dealing with similar learning challenges.

Chapter 8

Crossing Bridges

SUSTAINING FAMILY AND SCHOOL
ENGAGEMENTS TO SUPPORT ALL LEARNERS

Every morning, rain or shine, or anything in between, Mr. B, principal of PS X, stands tall outside of his large brick school building. As the students trudge up the ramp—sometimes completing a math sheet or reading a book—Mr. B solemnly, yet warmly, greets each one by name. Similarly, every parent receives a handshake or nod, a seemingly small moment. Each of these small moments of personal recognition, however, are Mr. B's act of thanks for entrusting their child to the care of the school and his assurance that their child is in an academically engaging and emotionally supportive environment.

With this final chapter, we review the five principles presented in the previous chapters with a focus on practical steps for enacting change at the classroom and school levels. We include additional suggestions to build further bridges to the larger community, such as establishing relationships with local libraries, after-school providers, and other community-based organizations.

To fully enact the five principles outlined in the previous chapters, there must be a strong school leader fully committed to providing tools, time, resources, and mentorship in building a school culture committed to authentic partnership with families. The job of a school principal has never been more challenging or more important than it is today.

Consider the myriad responsibilities of a school leader—creating schedules, leading instruction, managing staff, tending the facilities, addressing student issues, complying with regulations, to name a few (Tobin, 2014). Yet to truly establish a successful school, school leaders must consider how to imbue trust, collaboration, respect, adaptation, and celebration within their school to create successful bridges between community, home, and school.

To highlight the ways these principles interact and are important at the school level, we share a snapshot of a school whose leader, teachers, and staff identify supporting parents, and in particular families whose children struggle with literacy, as a critical school goal.

Public School X is a PK–8 school in an large northeastern city. With a population of just over seven hundred students who are largely of Hispanic or African American descent and who mostly qualify for free or reduced lunch, several of the issues that often afflict large urban schools—lack of resources, high teacher turnover, mandated initiatives from district or city officials—feel absent from its hallways.

Glimpses through classroom doorways afford views of students using technology to access differentiated reading supports as teachers facilitate small groups or literacy stations. Bulletin boards showcase project-based learning tasks that create connections between core subject areas through a student-selected issue or problem. Teacher teams collaborate actively to analyze student work, refine curricula, and communicate frequently with families around individual student goals.

A shared sense of ownership and pride—one that is balanced between the school leaders, teachers, students, and their families—is both deeply felt and clearly evident through a bright mural outside of the main office that proclaims the school's core values: open-mindedness, community, and dedication. In the following sections, we share reflections from the school and its leader, Mr. B, to provide insight into a principal's thinking and policy to support bridges between school and community.

IMPORTANCE OF TRUST

Building trusting relationships within a school is critical. Henderson and Mapp (2002) stress the importance of building authentic, welcoming, responsive relationships with families to support all learning. From a study of over two hundred family members, Tschannen-Moran (2014) found

> Whether parents perceived that they had a voice and could influence school decisions and whether their children felt a sense of belonging influenced parents' trust in the school to a greater extent than contextual conditions such as poverty status, school size, diverse ethnic composition, and school level. This suggests that school leaders can build and sustain parent trust by aligning policies and practices to be responsive to the needs of parents and to reduce the sense of vulnerability they perceived in parent-school relationship. (p. 64)

This study of the interconnectivity of trust between all school stakeholders (principal, teacher, students, families) reported higher levels of trust between and among stakeholders. "A principal who is trusted can be the glue that holds a school community together" (p. 59). School leaders play a critical role in whether or not families feel welcomed and valued or discouraged and dismissed.

Even when schools include the rhetoric of parent engagement in mission statements, families assess a school by the day-to-day actions and words of school leaders. For example, through interviews and focus groups with families, Barr and Saltmarsh (2014) learned that parents identify visibility, access, and communication practices as key components in leaders who authentically engage families. "The parents spoke of effective leaders as those predisposed to challenge deficit views held by some school personnel about parents and communities" (p. 499).

Principal Connection

Mr. B discusses developing trust through communication

Every single morning I'm outside of the school. That to me is the most important kind of communication. You know, parents are going to work and they'll stop by when they drop their child off and they'll speak to me, or they'll ask a question, and they'll know that I can at least guide them in the right direction if I can't give them the answer. I don't want them to feel like they have to set up a meeting. You hear that at many schools, where parents say, "I have to set up a meeting with the principal but I can't even enter the school." That's not where we are coming from.

I've had a parent come up and say, "Mr. B, I just wanted to say I know that I work and it's hard for me to get into the building, but it's almost as if the type of communication I get from the teacher and school means I'm in the classroom twenty-four hours a day." That to me is the biggest compliment. Because the parent know what's going on, they know how to help their child, and we the school have to work from that. It's so powerful.

COMMUNICATION AS THE KEY FOR COLLABORATION

In *Beyond the Bake Sale: The Essential Guide to Family-School Partnerships*, Henderson, Mapp, Johnson, and Davies (2007) present four different models of school–family partnerships, from most restrictive to most open. They characterize the Fortress School as one that views parents as trouble and the school's role as the redemptive institution in the neighborhood. Next is the Come-If-We-Call School, where families are welcome when they can be of service to the school and the student.

There is the Open-Door School, where families are invited to take a more active role in established organizations such as the PTA. Finally, they describe the Partnership School, which embraces family and community. As evident from the descriptions, the Partnership School views families as collaborators rather than viewers or even consumers. In chapter 3, we discussed the importance of building collaborative relationships with families along with strategies to enhance school events such as parent-teacher conferences and report cards. The school leader plays a critical role in establishing and sustaining those practices across a building. Mr. B's comments in the following Principle Connections illustrate this.

Principal Connection

There is a lot of discussion around how to best support teachers to work with families. There's a lot of the research we've read as a school that shows us that when we have our parents on our side, we will see greater academic growth. We can take that from early childhood all the way to the upper grades. Sometimes that means we have a lot of hard discussions. I'll meet with teachers and ask, "What are you doing to make sure that parents are involved?" We don't want learning to be a mystery. We don't want parents who are waiting for progress reports and report cards. We don't want communication without transparency. If they don't know, then we are doing something wrong.

Principal Connection

I want parents to be part of the educational process, and what better way to make them part of the educational process than to share exactly what's going on. More importantly, we want parents to have some shared decision making. Whether you call it an SLT committee or you have parent councils or PTA, they are decision makers. Parents in our school will tell you some of the things we can improve, and since we are on the same team we want to get some consensus building and we want to get some of their great ideas. It works best when I try to take it from the perspective of a parent. How do I want to be treated? What information do I want to know about my son and daughter? And how can I be helpful in that process? If I can't answer those questions for our parents, we have to be better.

To help you think about your school's communication policies and practices, use the assessment tool in appendix 8.1. By tracking responses to the questions about the frequency, type, and impact of these practices, you can identify areas that you and your school can change or enhance.

SUSTAINING RESPECTFUL RELATIONSHIPS

In chapter 4, we shared how teachers honored the photographs and artifacts shared by families and in doing so developed deep, respectful personal relationships with parents as well as utilized out-of-school literacies as key links to support literacy instruction. To extend this relationship, schools that adopt a partnership stance (Henderson, Mapp, Johnson, & Davies, 2007) both invite parents to actively engage with the school day and also recognize the assets families contribute to education. This is particularly critical for families of struggling readers, who may, as discussed earlier, react emotionally to their children's difficulties and blame teachers, the school, or the principal.

Principal Connection

Parents will say, "Mr. B, I heard my child is having a difficult time. Is it possible that I can sit in the classroom?" We have our classrooms open. I've never come across a teacher who, when I say, "Miss Johnson wants to come into your class to observe," says no to the parent's request. Teachers are always saying, "Yes, absolutely," because they know that that's going to enhance their relationship with the family. They know that keeping classrooms open sends that message to little Johnny: "Hey, mom and my teacher are on board here."

ADAPTING TO SUPPORT STUDENTS AND FAMILIES

In chapter 5, we discussed the importance of flexibility and adaptability within a school's curriculum so that there is space for families and teachers to share information and build literacy activities that support students' academic growth and also acknowledge the interests and expertise of students and their families.

Principal Connection

I have a fifth grade teacher who uses the Remind app to send pictures of students at work and pictures of their completed work. So what better way to talk, when we live in such a fast-paced world, where a lot of our parents are more often than not working? It's not that they don't want to be involved. They want to be involved, but they also have to put some food on the table and support their families, which is commendable. It means that the school has to adapt, that we have to find other ways to make sure they are part of the process. Everyone has a smartphone now, so what better way to make sure you see your son or daughter in the classroom learning? You are getting a quick snapshot of what's going on so you can reinforce it at home.

BUILDING COMMUNITY THROUGH CELEBRATION

As important as it is for the principal to initiate and sustain schoolwide curricular and professional learning opportunities for teachers to better engage with families, it is equally important for the principal to model being an active reader. By demonstrating to her or his teachers, staff, families, and students that reading is important and relevant, the principal plays a pivotal role in creating a literacy-rich culture that supports all readers.

One strategy used by many leaders is developing a book-of-the-month or "community read" structure. One significant example of a community-wide reading selection is the One City, One Book program. In 1998, the Seattle Public Library initiated this program to create a citywide book club and discussion around a shared text. The idea has grown to over four hundred cities, according to the Library of Congress. The goals—shared discussion and opportunity for exploration and celebration—make sense for a school community as well as a political/geographic community.

In a school, a book is chosen for each month of the school year and is shared across the school. All teachers and school staff use the book to foster discussions at the developmentally appropriate level of their students. Families can be engaged in numerous ways, such as coming to school for read-alouds with children, by reading the book at home and using if for discussion, or even by collaborating with teachers in extending the ideas generated from the book discussions into action through a project or literary response.

Mallory Locke, a literacy coach at an urban school, created a detailed suggested outline of a series of community reads and activities. Textbox 8.1 is an example for grades K–3 from her "Community Reads Scope and Sequence," which features texts, topics, essential questions, and suggested activities. Similarly, she has created suggestions appropriate for grades 4–6 (textbox 8.2).

Textbox 8.1

September
(School Year Begins)

Text:
Exclamation Mark by Amy Krouse Rosenthal

Topics:
Inclusion, Community, Differences

Theme:
What makes you different helps you *make your mark!*

Questions to Consider as a Community:
What makes me unique?
How can we celebrate differences?
How will I *make my mark?*

Family Workshop Ideas:
Literacy Focused
Punctuation Flipbook Creation: Families will create sentence starters for practice with endings such as periods, exclamation marks, and question marks.

Community Focused
Making Our Mark Mural: Families will create SMART (specific, measurable, achievable, relevant, timely) goals for the school year on cutouts of exclamation marks, showcasing how each school member will do something to "make their mark" on a great school year.

Textbox 8.2

October
(Make a Difference Day, World Smile Day)

November
(Veteran's Day, Thanksgiving)

Text:
Wonder by R. J. Palacio

Topics:
Inclusion, Differences, Acceptance, Friendship

Theme:
True friendship comes in many forms.

Questions to Consider as a Community:
What makes me unique?
How can we celebrate differences?
What are the qualities of a true friendship?

Family Workshop Ideas:
Literacy Focused

Topics, Themes, and Tales "Wonder Wall": Families will work together to create a "wonder wall" featuring overarching topics and themes from the text. Families will share stories related to the themes from the text, highlighting the real-world relevance of the novel.

Community Focused

"What Unites Us" Friendship Quilt: Families will decorate quilt fabric tiles to showcase family values, favorite family activities, and significant beliefs. Quilt fabric tiles will be stitched together with the support of volunteer students and their families to create a single friendship quilt for display.

The "Community Reads Scope and Sequence" presents a useful outline of topics, themes, guiding questions, and suggested activities. Use this as a model or template toward thinking about a schoolwide approach to building literacy community. The full outline of topics can be found in appendix 8.3.

Principal Connection

I want to make sure that parents know exactly what's going on. All the things we do speak to the value we place on our parents. We value our community. I come from the frame of mind that the community defines who you are. If the community is saying you are a successful school, then you are a successful school. It's not just about reading and math scores. It's what our neighbors have to say about what we're about and the kind of experiences we create for our students and their families. That, to me, is the most important. Empowering parents empowers their voices, which they share outside of our school in the neighborhood. That's the greatest thing.

EXTENDING THE PRINCIPLES INTO THE COMMUNITY

After-School Programs

There have been discrepancies concerning the effects of after-school programs. Some findings illustrate positive associations between an after-school program and academic success, whereas other studies have yielded null or negative correlations (Grogan, Henrich, & Malikina, 2014; Mahoney, Lord, & Carryl, 2005). However, studies have consistently indicated that when academic success has had a positive association to an after-school program, the programs show a pattern of common characteristics (Grogan, Henrich, & Malikina, 2014; Mahoney, Lord, & Carryl, 2005; Sadler & Staulters, 2008; Sheldon, Arbreton, Hopkins, & Grossman, 2010).

According to the studies, characteristics of a high-quality after-school program associated with student academic achievement include student engagement, increased opportunity for participants to interact with books, provision of appropriate and consistent instructional structure, and regular attendance. High-quality indicators include read-alouds, book discussions, skill development, attention to vocabulary, and a coordinated process for providing professional development (Kremer, Maynard, Polanin, Vaughn, & Sarteschi, 2015; Sheldon, Arbreton, Hopkins, & Grossman, 2010). Additionally, according to Mahoney, Lord, and Carryl (2005), the participants must find the program appealing and enjoyable as well as challenging when these characteristics effectively balance the demands placed on the individuals in relationship to their existing abilities and interests.

There are two types of after-school programs that offer academic assistance: those that assist with homework assigned by the child's teacher that is connected to the school curriculum, and after-school programs that offer activities that provide academic enrichment and skill building that are not necessarily associated with or in coordination with the child's specific needs (Cosden, Morrison, Albanese, & Macias, 2001).

After-school programs offer the opportunity for struggling readers to get the extra help they need to succeed in an informal setting. Some of the programs work on a one-to-one basis with struggling readers, while other programs are designed to engage children in read-alouds and literacy activities in authentic ways. Programs can be offered by the school, local colleges, YMCAs, or other community-based organizations, all of which seek to provide a variety of programs that use literacy as a basis for other areas of study, such as sports, the arts, and STEM.

For families looking for an effective academic after-school program for their struggling readers, a number of things should be considered. Here are some questions you can discuss with the family to help them prepare to look at programs. Before going to visit a program, ask: Does the student work well in larger groups? With fewer children? In a one-on-one setting? Is the student comfortable in groups of children from his or her own school? Is he or she comfortable adapting to a new or different setting other than the day school he or she attends? What are your goals in having your struggling reader attend an after-school program? It is essential that families are clear about expectations of any program.

Two teachers facilitated an after-school, college-based tutoring program. The Literacy Space program was a two-semester practicum course for teachers pursuing their advanced certification in literacy. Participating children attended the program once a week for seventy-five-minute sessions, twenty-five sessions in total. Included in the program structure was a room for the tutor and family member to have "doorway conversations" at the end of each session, during which the child's progress was discussed from an asset-based framework. At the end of each of the two semesters, the family received a letter from the child's tutor describing the literacy strengths the child showcased as well as areas in need of development. The tutor's letter also suggested texts, websites, and strategies the family and child could use together to support continued growth.

The facilitators found that many parents and caregivers waited for their children while they were engaged with tutors in the Literacy Space, an opportunity our graduate students capitalized on by developing and delivering family workshops. Topics included questioning during television watching, family literacy games, how to select an appropriate book, read-aloud strategies, and even how to engage in parent–teacher conferences from a more informed and empowered position.

While one small group of tutors led the workshops, participating students worked in small groups with another tutor. Families were extremely pleased with each workshop and expressed that not only did they find them valuable and easy to attend, but they more importantly felt valued as participants in their struggling readers' learning. Tutors provided handouts in multiple languages, and whenever possible the workshop were also translated, sometimes by one of the participating family members.

The Literacy Space also created nights of celebration and literacy games for families of participating children. Tutors created games that targeted both interests and gaps in children's literacy development, and families who played the games noticed the informal ways children were learning and developing literacy strategies through active learning.

Participants' final sessions in the Literacy Space celebrated their progress through student performances of readers' theater pieces, graphic novels, plays, poetry, comedy, or informational texts, highlighting all they learned around their interests and abilities acquired through their participation.

Evaluating After-School Programs

To support families in considering different after-school programs' curricula and approaches, the following checklist has been developed (drawing on EarlyEducationMatters.org; Kelly, n.d.; Rowley, 2017; Smith, 2015). Recommend this checklist for each after-school program visited.

Checklist to Evaluate an After-School Program

Name of Program:_____ Affiliation: <u>e.g., school, college,</u>
                                                          <u>nonprofit</u>
Contact Person:_____ Phone #_____

_____

Question	Answer	Are you comfortable with this response?	Evidence or questions you have.
What is the staff-to-student ratio? (ideally it would be fifteen or fewer students to each staff member)			
Does the program director have formal education and professional preparation to manage the program?			

Do instructional staff have formal education or professional preparation to teach?

Do they have a parent/family handbook? Does it include a mission statement and philosophy?

Do they have a consistent program schedule? Review this for themes and project-based activities, including time for physical play, academic opportunities, and homework support. Do program activities change often enough so children don't get bored?

How are children encouraged to try new activities and build new skills? Will my child be learning something new every day?

Is there someone available to help my child with homework?

If the program is school based, does it connect with the school's teachers or align itself with the curriculum? If so, how does that work?

Do I feel my child will be safe and comfortable here?

Watch a class in action:

Do they treat children with respect and listen to them?

Do they seem to know each child's interests, personality, culture, home language?

Do they help children learn by giving them opportunities to think for themselves?

Do they use positive techniques to guide their behavior?

Are there a variety of materials and activities to engage children?

How does staff handle discipline?

OTHER RESOURCES TO CONSIDER

Sometimes budgetary limitations make reaching our goals for crossing literacy bridges difficult. Not all schools have the financial ability to support all our efforts. We need to be creative in considering how to bring families and schools together to support the achievement of children struggling with literacy. We have found several funding sources to look to in order to support our efforts and consider creative ways to enhance literacy programs. As always, funding requirements and deadlines change.

Library Resources

Libraries are not just about books in the twenty-first century. Most local libraries now offer online resources, such as audio books and videos. Kanopy (www.kanopystreaming.com) provides streaming of movies, documentaries, and short informational pieces, accessed for free through libraries on laptops, tablets, and phones. These resources create valuable access points for curriculum connections. This is just one example of the ways libraries can be partners in supporting educational goals shared by teachers and families.

Lopez, Caspe, and McWilliams (2016) provide excellent resources to promote the ways libraries can support families in literacy growth. They describe three ways that libraries support families. Broadly, they posit libraries are supportive in three domains: as people, as a place, and as a platform. Libraries' support as people means that librarians play a critical role in meeting with families, understanding their needs, and collaborating with them to plan meaningful programs to support the literacy development of all family members.

In addition, librarians also guide families in accessing the ever-growing multimedia resources available. As a place, libraries serve as a physical space for families and community to meet and deepen connections. Libraries as a platform acknowledge the great growth in the forms and types of literacies as well as how libraries can form a nexus for networking and initiating programs that benefit the educational outcomes of community members.

In their work with librarians and libraries across the country, Lopez, Caspe, and McWilliams (2016) synthesize and describe "5Rs" that illustrate particular ways libraries support family literacy engagement. These include reaching out, as libraries and librarians actively seek families to promote their programs; raising up, referring to providing access and voice to families; reinforcing, to sustain the habits and growth of families' new practices; relating, by providing services to support interpersonal and networking opportunities and growth; and finally, reimagining, by extending and supporting the whole family and community. For more detailed descriptions of the innovative approaches libraries are exploring, see "Want to Know More?" at the end of this chapter.

Understanding the changing roles of libraries is important for teachers. Take time to investigate the libraries in your community. In what ways do their programs align with yours? How can you partner with the library to provide additional resources and support for your students and their families?

Grants

Lowe's donates up to five million dollars per year to K–12 public and charter schools through its Toolbox for Education programs. It provides help to educators and parent groups to upgrade technology, renovate facilities, create reading gardens, and establish parent involvement centers. For a grant application and to read about funded projects, visit www.toolboxforeducation. com.

The P. Buckley Moss Foundation for Children's Education supports grants of up to $1,000. They fund new or evolving programs that integrate the arts into educational program. According to their website, "The purpose is to aid and support teachers who wish to establish an effective learning tool using the arts in teaching children who learn differently." For more information, go to their website at mossfoundation.org.

Target recognizes how difficult it is to fund learning opportunities outside the classroom. They fund field trips up to $700 to schools across the nation. Think of opportunities struggling readers and their families together could benefit from outside learning opportunities. To apply, go to https://corporate. target.com/corporate-responsibility/grants/field-trip-grants.

The National Education Association recognizes educators frequently need outside resources to engage in meaningful professional development due to limited district funding. Through their Learning & Leadership grants, they support the professional development of NEA members by providing grants to participate in high-quality professional development but also to fund collegial study, lesson plan development, and mentoring experiences. Think of opportunities to work with colleagues to establish strong family–school partnerships for children struggling with literacy acquisition. For information, go to their website: http://www.neafoundation.org/pages/ learning-leadership-grants.

James Patterson partnered with Scholastic to provide grants to school libraries. Applications may be submitted by teachers, librarians, administrators, or parents on behalf of any U.S. school that services students in grades Pre-K through 12. Applications must be made online by completing and submitting the application form found at http://www.scholastic.com/pattersonpartnership/. Awards range from $1,000 to $10,000 and also include Scholastic Bonus Points. Consider the materials the library may be missing that would enhance and support your work with children struggling with literacy acquisition.

SUMMARY

Building bridges and caring for the relationships between teachers and families is one of our essential roles as educators. Nurturing this relationship through difficult times to build the resilience and strengths of students is special and important work. We acknowledge that the roadway across the bridge may be shaky and takes courage to cross. We hope the principles we have discussed, the strategies we have identified, and the suggestions we have made to move forward will be helpful in your work with the families of struggling readers.

You may recall completing a self-assessment of your knowledge in areas of supporting families in chapter 1. Through reading this book, exploring ideas with colleagues, and hopefully trying out strategies and suggestions, you have developed a greater knowledge and sense of self-efficacy in working with families of struggling readers. We invite you to reflect on your growth and develop new goals with this exercise once again (appendix 8.2).

Want to Know More?

Books to inform schoolwide family engagement:

- Henderson, Mapp, Johnson, and Davies's (2007) *Beyond the Bake Sale: The Essential Guide to Family-School Partnerships*.
- Hong, S. (2011). *A Cord of Three Strands: A New Approach to Parent Engagement in Schools*. Cambridge, MA: Harvard Education Press.

Books providing more ways to implement school-wide family engagement in literacy:

- Allen's (2007) *Creating Welcoming Schools: A Practical Guide to Home-School Partnerships with Diverse Families*.
- Dunsmore, K., & Fisher, D. (Eds.). (2010). *Bringing literacy home*. Newark, DE: International Literacy Association.

Websites with monthly newsletters to explore:

- Global Family Research Project, https://globalfrp.org/.
- See newsletter *Expanding the Potential of Anywhere, Anytime Learning*: https://studentsatthecenterhub.org/resource/expanding-opportunity-the-potential-of-anywhere-anytime-learning-fine-june-2014-newsletter/.

Policy briefs to guide collaborations beyond school:

- "Public Libraries: A Vital Space for Family Engagement," http://www.ala.org/pla/sites/ala.org.pla/files/content/initiatives/familyengagement/Public-Libraries-A-Vital-Space-for-Family-Engagement_HFRP-PLA_August-2-2016.pdf.
- *Family Engagement Brief* (Spring 2014), http://www.familieslearning.org/pdf/NCFL_Family_Engagement_Brief_.pdf.

APPENDIX 8.1

Appendix 8.1 Tool for Practice: Communicating with Families

Communicating with Families
Our school values parents in the following ways:

A team of teachers or school staff schedules meetings to meet with parents to share school business, academic updates, etc.

Daily   Weekly   Monthly   Once a Marking Period   Once a School Year

A team of parents develops agendas for meetings with school staff regarding home interests, concerns, and feedback.

Daily   Weekly   Monthly   Once a Marking Period   Once a School Year

Invitations are extended to parents seeking attendance at classroom publishing parties, project sharings, book clubs, etc.

Daily   Weekly   Monthly   Once a Marking Period   Once a School Year

Invitations are extended to parents seeking attendance at gradewide events, field trips, programs, etc.

Daily   Weekly   Monthly   Once a Marking Period   Once a School Year

Invitations are extended to parents seeking attendance at schoolwide presentations, workshops, holiday programs, etc.

Daily   Weekly   Monthly   Once a Marking Period   Once a School Year

Workshops are delivered that provide academic enrichment or remedial support training for parents.

Daily   Weekly   Monthly   Once a Marking Period   Once a School Year

Parents and teachers collaborate on workshops to include teachers, parents, and students in shared learning.

Daily   Weekly   Monthly   Once a Marking Period   Once a School Year

Teachers or grade teams and parents meet to develop opportunities for volunteering or assistance within the classroom.

Daily   Weekly   Monthly   Once a Marking Period   Once a School Year

Teachers, school leadership, and parents meet to collaboratively set and monitor the school's academic, social, and community goals.

Daily   Weekly   Monthly   Once a Marking Period   Once a School Year

Our school connects with the community in the following ways:

Community programming information is disseminated through paper (flyers, pamphlets, etc.) and digital (email, apps) communication between the school and home.

Daily   Weekly   Monthly   Once a Marking Period   Once a School Year

*Teachers, school staff, parents, and community members meet to identify
opportunities to create events, programming, or volunteering that connects school
and community.*

Daily   Weekly   Monthly   Once a Marking Period   Once a School Year

*In-school workshops connect teachers, parents, and community-based service
providers through a common theme or shared problem.*

Daily   Weekly   Monthly   Once a Marking Period   Once a School Year

APPENDIX 8.2

Appendix 8.2 Supporting Families of Struggling Readers: Teacher Self-Assessment

Directions: After exploring the five principles in this book, take a moment to consider
how you will now approach the following practices.

1: Not able to apply yet	1	2	3	4	5
2: Curious to try
3: Will take steps to try
4: Definitely will try
5: Part of my current practice and eager to expand

1. Use surveys to learn about struggling readers'
   interests, personality traits, and literacy histories.

2. Use surveys to learn about families' hopes and
   concerns about their struggling readers' educational
   experiences.

3. Initiate informal conversations with families at drop-
   off, pickup, or other school events.

4. Develop and cultivate trust with family members.

5. Demonstrate understanding of diverse family
   compositions, cultures, and values.

6. Include opportunities to integrate family stories into
   curriculum.

7. Provide opportunities for families to learn about
   literacy practices to try at home.

8. Thoughtfully and purposefully plan and implement
   family literacy events that meet families' needs.

9. Conduct parent–teacher conferences that build on
   students' literacy strengths.

10. Use accessible language in parent–teacher
    conferences and in report cards.

11. Effectively communicate with families information about struggling readers' literacy strengths and challenges.

12. Draw upon growing knowledge of high-quality children's books to support empathy and understanding of diverse families.

13. Utilize and connect families to community literacy resources.

14. Advocate for families within and outside of schools.

APPENDIX 8.3

Appendix 8.3 Community Reads: Monthly Read-Aloud Scope and Sequence

Kindergarten–Grade 3 Map

September (School Year Begins)	October (Make a Difference Day, World Smile Day)	November (Veteran's Day, Thanksgiving)	December (Holidays)	January (MLK Jr. Day)
Text: *Exclamation Mark* by Amy Krouse Rosenthal	**Text:** *Enemy Pie* by Derek Munson	**Text:** *How to Heal a Broken Wing* by Bob Graham	**Text:** *Those Shoes* by Maribeth Boelts	**Text:** *A Sweet Smell of Roses* by Angela Johnson
Topics: Inclusion, Community, Differences	**Topics:** Friendship, Making Assumptions	**Topics:** Selflessness, Service	**Topics:** Making Sacrifices, Everyday Heroism	**Topics:** Leadership, Bravery
Theme: What makes you different helps you *make your mark!*	**Theme:** There is more that unites us than divides us.	**Theme:** Kindness starts with you: If not now, when? If not us, who?	**Theme:** Giving to others is a gift we give ourselves.	**Theme:** Doing what is right, even when it isn't easy, is what makes a great leader.
Questions to Consider as a Community: What makes me unique? How can we celebrate differences? How will I *make my mark*?	**Questions to Consider as a Community:** What are the ingredients in a good friendship? How do we find common ground?	**Questions to Consider as a Community:** What needs do we see in our community? How can we make a difference in the lives of others? How does helping others help ourselves?	**Questions to Consider as a Community:** What is the difference between want and need? How do we help create a more equitable world for everyone?	**Questions to Consider as a Community:** What are the qualities of a great leader? What does bravery look and sound like?
Family Workshop Ideas: **Literacy Focused** Punctuation Flipbook Creation: Families will create sentence starters for practice with endings such as periods, exclamation marks, and question marks.	**Family Workshop Ideas:** **Literacy Focused** Compare/Contrast Signal Word Cloud Creation: Families will create word clouds for language that supports comparing and contrasting.	**Family Workshop Ideas:** **Literacy Focused** Graphic Novel Study: Families will generate questions to support readers in combining text and images to make meaning.	**Family Workshop Ideas:** **Literacy Focused** Picking "Just Right Books" That Fit: Families will participate in a workshop exploring reading levels, lexile scores, and tips for selecting texts.	**Family Workshop Ideas:** **Literacy Focused** Historical Graphic Novels: Families will work together to create a graphic novel depicting an important event in the family time line.
Community Focused Making Our Mark Mural: Families will create goals for the school year on cutouts of exclamation marks, showcasing how each school member will do something to "make a mark" on a great school year.	**Community Focused** "What Unites Us" Friendship Quilt: Families will decorate quilt fabric tiles to showcase family values, favorite family activities, etc.	**Community Focused** School/Grade-Level Service Project: Families and teachers will work together to identify a service project to enact as a grade level or as a school	**Community Focused** Everyday Heroes Theater: Families will draft and perform scenes featuring "everyday heroes" from family experiences, the school context, or the community at large.	**Community Focused** Sweeter School Rules Rewrite: Students, families, teachers, and school leaders will revisit school rules and draft addendums to language that spotlight inclusivity, respect, and a culture of community.

February	March	April	May	June
(Black History Month)	*(International Women's Day)*	*(National Poetry Month)*	*(Mothers' Day)*	*(Summer Begins)*
Text: *Mufaro's Beautiful Daughters* by John Steptoe	**Text:** *She Persisted* by Chelsea Clinton	**Text:** *The Book with No Pictures* by B. J. Novak	**Text:** *Horton Hatches the Egg* by Dr. Seuss	**Text:** *Summer Days and Nights* by Wong Herbert Lee
Topics: Making Hard Decisions	**Topics:** Persistence, Innovation	**Topics:** Purposes of Reading, Language, Expressing Ourselves	**Topics:** Love, Families, Responsibility	**Topics:** Exploration, Creativity
Themes: Everyone deserves to be treated fairly.	**Theme:** Use grit to persist in the face of obstacles.	**Theme:** Language can inform us, persuade us, and *delight us.*	**Theme:** Families come in all shapes and forms	**Questions to Consider as a Community:** What can I explore and learn this summer?
Questions to Consider as a Community: What characteristics make a person special?	**Questions to Consider as a Community:** How can we use our talents to persist for those in need?	**Questions to Consider as a Community:** Why do we read? How can we use language to express ourselves?	**Questions to Consider as a Community:** What makes a family?	**Family Workshop Ideas:** **Literacy Focused** Setting SMART goals for summer (specific, measurable, actionable, realistic, timely)
Family Workshop Ideas: **Literacy Focused** Story Elements Stations: Families participate in a station rotation, receiving supports and enrichment materials for setting, characters, or plot.	**Family Workshop Ideas:** **Literacy Focused** Family Biographies: Families will work together to create short biographical picture books about important members of their families.	**Family Workshop Ideas:** **Literacy Focused** Reading for Joy: Families will celebrate language through the sharing of tongue twisters, poetry, and more	**Family Workshop Ideas:** **Literacy Focused** Journaling for Organization and Reflection: Families will explore ways to use logs, journals, and diaries to support organization, responsibility, and reflection.	**Community Focused** Summer enrichment support (free city trips, city programs, etc.).
Community Focused Storytelling Circle: Families share favorite folktales, fables, or myths within classrooms, grade levels, or as a school.	**Community Focused** Crafting for a Cause School Craft Fair: Families will work together to craft or create a piece for auction at a school craft fair, the proceeds of which will support a charity identified by the classroom, grade team, or school at large.	**Community Focused** Poetry Slam: Families will participate in a poetry slam featuring works written by students, teachers, and families.	**Community Focused** Egg Baby Project: Families will care for an "egg baby," working together to complete care logs detailing the responsibilities enacted by the student and his or her family to care for the egg baby.	

Grades 4–6 Map

September	December
(School Year Begins)	*(Holidays)*
October	**January**
(Make a Difference Day, World Smile Day)	*(MLK Jr. Day)*
November	**February**
(Veteran's Day, Thanksgiving)	*(Black History Month)*

Text:
Wonder by R. J. Palacio

Topics:
Inclusion, Differences, Acceptance, Friendship

Theme:
True friendship comes in many forms.

Questions to Consider as a Community:
What makes me unique?
How can we celebrate differences?
What are the qualities of a true friendship?

Family Workshop Ideas:
Literacy Focused
Topics, Themes, and Tales "Wonder Wall": Families will work together to create a "wonder wall" featuring overarching topics and themes from the text. Families will share tales related to the themes from the text, highlighting the real-world relevance of the novel.

Community Focused
"What Unites Us" Friendship Quilt: Families will decorate quilt fabric tiles to showcase family values, favorite family activities, etc.

Text:
Esperanza Rising by Pam Muñoz Ryan

Topics:
Persistence, Overcoming Obstacles, Grief, Gratitude

Theme:
It's not about starting over, but beginning anew.

Questions to Consider as a Community:
How do our perspectives affect the way we combat challenges?
How much influence does our past have on our future?

Family Workshop Ideas:
Literacy Focused
Letters to Our Future Selves: Families will participate in letter writing workshops, describing their current perspectives, hopes, and dreams for the future. Letters will be enclosed in time capsules, which will be revisited at the beginning of the following school year.

Community Focused
"Revisiting Roots" Family History Project: Families will create representations detailing family histories (countries of origin, notable family members, etc.) and share within the class, grade level, or schoolwide community.

March
(International Women's Day)
April
(National Poetry Month)
May
(Mothers' Day)
June
(Summer Begins)

Text:
Maniac Magee by Jerry Spinelli

Topics:
Friendship, Family, Homelessness, Justice, Equity

Theme:
The lines between friends, family, and home are more connected than they seem.

Questions to Consider as a Community:
What makes a family?
What makes a home?
How do responsibility, care, and love collide?

Family Workshop Ideas:
Literacy Focused
Legends and Tall Tales Theater: Families will read legends and tall tales from around the world, crafting tableaux or short scenes to reenact the stories for classmates, other members of the grade level, or the school community.

Community Focused
"What Makes a Family" Photo Definition Project: Using the theme from *Maniac Magee* that a family is what you make it, students will share photographs documenting the different individuals who are considered to be family. Students will also create photo captions describing why the person is like a family member, showcasing the different definitions and thematic connections of the term *family*.

References

Ada, A. F. (1995). *My name is Maria Isabel.* New York: Atheneum Books for Young Readers.

Ada, A. F. (2003). *A magical encounter: Latino children's literature in the classroom.* Boston: Allyn and Bacon.

Afflerbach, P. (2017). *Understanding and using reading assessment, K–12* (3rd ed.). ASCD.

Afflerbach, P. P., & Johnston, P. H. (1993). Writing language arts report cards: Eleven teachers' conflicts of knowing and communicating. *Elementary School Journal, 94*(1), 73–86.

Al-Hazza, T. C. (2010). Motivating disengaged readers through multicultural children's literature. *New England Reading Association Journal, 45*(2), 63–68.

Allen, J. (2007). *Creating welcoming schools: A practical guide to home-school partnerships with diverse families.* New York: Teachers College Press.

Allington, R. L. (2011). *What really matters for struggling readers* (3rd ed.). Boston: Pearson.

Alvarez, M. C., Armstrong, S. L., Elish-Piper, L., Matthews, M. W., & Risko, V. J. (2009). Deconstructing the construct of "struggling reader": Standing still or transforming expectations and instruction. *American Reading Forum Annual Yearbook 29.*

Alvarez, S. (2014). Emergent bilingual youth as language brokers for homework in immigrant families. *Language Arts, 91*(5), 326–39.

Amatea, E. S. (2013). *Building culturally responsive family-school relationships* (2nd ed.). Boston: Pearson.

Auerbach, E. (1989). Toward a social-contextual approach to family literacy. *Harvard Educational Review, 59*(2), 165–81.

Auerbach, E. (1995a). Deconstructing the discourse of strengths in family literacy. *Journal of Reading Behavior, 27*(4), 643–61.

Auerbach, E. (1995b). Which way for family literacy: Intervention or empowerment? In L. M. Morrow (Ed.), *Family literacy: Connections in schools and communities* (pp. 11–28). Newark, DE: International Reading Association.

Aukerman, M. (2015). How should readers develop across time? Mapping change *without* a deficit perspective. *Language Arts, 93*(1), 55–62.

Bailey, J. M., & Guskey, T. (2000). *Implementing student-led conferences*. Thousand Oaks, CA: Corwin Press.

Baird, A. S. (2015). Beyond the greatest hits: a counterstory of english learner parent involvement. *School Community Journal, 25*(2), 153.

Baker, L. (2003). The role of parents in motivating struggling readers. *Reading and Writing Quarterly, 19*(1), 87–106.

Barone, D. (2011). Welcoming families: A parent literacy project in a linguistically rich, high-poverty school. *Early Childhood Education Journal, 38*(5), 377–84.

Barr, J., & Saltmarsh, S. (2014). "It all comes down to the leadership": The role of the school principal in fostering parent-school engagement. *Educational Management Administration & Leadership, 42*(4), 491–505.

Battle-Bailey, L. (2004). Interactive homework for increasing parent involvement and student reading achievement. *Childhood Education, 81*(1), 36–40.

Beaty, J. J. (1997). *Building bridges with multicultural picture books for children 3–5.* Upper Saddle River, NJ: Prentice Hall.

Berlack, A., & Moyenda, S. (2001). *Taking it personally: Racism in the classroom from kindergarten to college.* Philadelphia: Temple University Press.

Bildner, P. (2004). *Twenty-one elephants.* New York: Simon and Schuster.

Bishop, R. S. (1990). Mirrors, windows, and sliding glass doors. *Perspectives, 6*(3), ix–xi.

Block, C. Lacina, J., Israel, S. E., Caylor, N., Massey, D., & Kirby, K. (2009). Examining literacy report cards. *New England Reading Association Journal, 45*(1), 34.

Briggs, N., Jalongo, M. R., & Brown, L. (1997). Working with families of young children: Our history and future goals. In J. P. Isenberg & M. Rench Jolango (Eds.), *Major trends and issues in early childhood education: Challenges, controversies and insights* (pp. 56–70). New York: Teachers College Press.

Brown, A. L., Harris, M., Jacobson, A., & Trotti, J. (2014). Parent teacher education connection: Preparing preservice teachers for family engagement. *Teacher Educator, 49*, 133–51.

Bruner, J. (1986). Two modes of thought. *Actual minds, possible worlds*, 11-43.

Cadwell, L. B. (1997). *Bringing learning to life: The Reggio approach to early childhood education.* New York: Teachers College Press.

Cairney, T. H. (2002). Bridging home and school literacy: In search of transformative approaches to curriculum. *Early Child Development and Care, 17*(2), 153–72.

Campano, G. (2005). The second class: Providing spaces in the margin. *Language Arts, 82*(3), 186–94.

Campano, G., Ghiso, M. P., Yee, M., & Pantoja, A. (2013). Toward community research and coalitional literacy practices for educational justice. *Language Arts, 90*(5), 314–26.

Caspe, M. (2003). *Family literacy: A review of programs and critical perspectives.* Harvard Family Research Project, Cambridge, MA. Retrieved from www.finenetwork.org

Catapano, S. (2006). Teaching in urban schools: Mentoring pre-service teachers to apply advocacy strategies. *Mentoring and Tutoring, 14*(1), 81–96.

Chang-Wells, G. L., & Wells, G. (1992). *Constructing knowledge together: Classrooms as centers of inquiry and literacy*. Heinemann Educational Books.

Chavkin, N. F. (2005, Winter). Strategies for preparing educators to enhance the involvement of diverse families in their children's education. *Multicultural Education*, 16–20.

Choi, Y. (2003). *The name jar*. New York: Dragonfly Books.

Clay, M. (1980). *Reading: The patterning of complex behavior* (2nd ed.). Auckland, NZ: Heinemann.

Cliatt, M. J. P., & Shaw, J. M. (1988). The storytime exchange: Ways to enhance it. *Childhood Education, 64*(5), 293–298.

Comber, B. (1996). *Professional bandwagons and local discursive effects: Reporting the literate student*. Paper presented at the Annual Meeting of the Australian Association for Research in Education. (ERIC Document Reproduction Service No. ED 444136).

Comber, B. (2013). Schools as meeting places: Critical and inclusive literacies in changing local environments. *Language Arts, 90*(5), 361–71.

Compton-Lilly, C. (2003). *Reading families: The literate lives of urban children*. New York: Teachers College Press.

Compton-Lilly, C. (2005). Sounding out: A pervasive cultural model of reading. *Language Arts, 82*(6), 441–51.

Compton-Lilly, C. (2015). Reading lessons from Martin: A case study of one African American student. *Language Arts, 92*(6), 401–11.

Cooper, J. D., Chard, D., & Kiger, N. D. (2006). *The struggling reader: Interventions that work*. Education Review/Reseñas Educativas. New York: Scholastic.

Corno, L. (1996). Homework is a complicated thing. *Educational Researcher, 25*, 27–29.

Cosden, M., Morrison, G., Albanese, A. L., & Macias, S. (2001). When homework is not home work: After-school programs for homework assistance. *Educational Psychologist, 36*(3), 211–21.

Craig, S., Hull, K., Haggart, A. G., & Crowder, E. (2001). Storytelling addressing the literacy needs of diverse learners. *Teaching Exceptional Children, 33*(5), 46–51.

Cumming, M. (2006). *Three names of me*. Park Ridge, IL: Albert Whitman.

Cunningham, K. E. (2015). *Story: Still the heart of literacy learning*. Portland, ME: Stenhouse.

Dail, A. R., & Payne, R. L. (2010). Recasting the role of family involvement in early literacy development: A response to the NELP report. *Educational Researcher, 39*(4), 330–33.

Dana, N. F., & Lynch-Brown, C. (1993). Children's literature: Preparing pre-service teachers for the multicultural classroom. *Action in Teacher Education, 14*(4), 45–51.

Daniels, H. (2017). The curious classroom. Portsmouth, NH: Heinemann.

DeCastro-Ambrosetti, D., & Cho, G. (2005). Do parents value education? Teachers' perceptions of minority parents. *Multicultural Education 13*(2), 44–46.

DeFauw, D. L., & Burton, E. L. (2009). Listening to the parents of struggling readers: An analysis of a parent focus group. *Michigan Reading Journal, 41*(1), 30–38.

de la Peña, M. (2015). *Last stop on Market Street*. New York: G.P. Putnam's Son.

Delgado-Gaitan, C., & Trueba, E. T. (1991). *Crossing cultural borders: Education for immigrant families in America*. London: Falmer Press.

Dennis, D. V., & Margarella, E. E. (2017). Family literacy nights: How participation impacts reading attitudes. *Literacy Practice and Research, 42*(3), 45–50.

Department of Health and Human Services Administration for Children and Families. (2016). *Head Start Program performance standards*. 45 CFR Chapter XIII. RIN 0970-AC63. Retrieved from https://eclkc.ohs.acf.hhs.gov/hslc/hs/docs/hspss-final.pdf

Dotger, B. H., Harris, S., Maher, M., & Hansel, A. (2011). Exploring the emotional geographies of parent–teacher candidate interactions: An emerging signature pedagogy. *The Teacher Educator, 46*(3), 208-230.

Dreher, M. J. (2003). Motivating struggling readers by tapping the potential of information books. *Reading and Writing Quarterly, 19*(1), 25–38.

Dudley-Marling, C. (2000). *A family affair: When school troubles come home*. Portsmouth, NH: Heinemann.

Dudley-Marling, C. (2009). Home-school literacy connections: The perceptions of African-American and immigrant ESL parents in two urban communities. *Teachers College Record, 111*(7), 1713–53.

Dudley-Marling, C., & Lucas, K. (2009). Pathologizing the language and culture of poor children. *Language Arts, 86*(5), 362–370.

Duke, N. (2014, November 20). Teaching tips: U.S. Dept. of Ed. calls for strong home/school connection. *Literacy Daily Blog*. Retrieved from https://www.literacyworldwide.org/blog/literacy-daily/2014/ 11/20/u-s-dept-of-ed-calls-for-strong-home-school-connection.

Duke, N. K., & Purcell-Gates, V. (2003). Genres at home and at school: Bridging the known to the new. *Reading Teacher, 57*(1), 30–37.

Dunsmore, K., Ordonez-Jasis, R., & Herrera, G. (2013). Welcoming their worlds: Rethinking literacy instruction through community mapping. *Language Arts, 90*(5), 327–38.

Durán, L. (2016). Revisiting family message journals: Audience and biliteracy development in a first-grade ESL classroom. *Language Arts, 93*(5), 354–65.

Dweck, C. S. (2007). The perils and promises of praise. *Educational Leadership, 65*(2), 34–39.

Eder, D. J. (2007). Bringing Navajo storytelling practices into schools: The importance of maintaining cultural integrity. *Anthropology & Education Quarterly, 38*(3), 278–96.

Edwards, P. A., Pleasants, M. H., & Franklin, S. H. (1999). *A path to follow: Learning to listen to parents*. Portsmouth, NH: Heinemann.

Edwards, P. A., Paratore, J. R., & Roser, N. (2009). Family literacy: Recognizing cultural significance. In L. M. Morrow, R. Rueda, & D. Lapp (Eds.), *Handbook of research on literacy and diversity* (pp. 77–96). New York: Guilford Press.

Endrizzi, C. K. (2008). *Becoming teammates: Teachers and families as literacy partners*. Urbana, IL: National Council of Teachers of English.

Endrizzi, C. K. (2016). Photos as bridges into hidden literacy lives. In R. Meyers & K. Whitmore (Eds.), *Reclaiming early childhood literacies* (pp. 240–43). New York: Routledge.

Engel, D. (1999). *Josephina hates her name*. New York: Feminist Press.

Enz, B. J. (1995). Strategies for promoting parental support for emergent literacy. *Reading Teacher, 46*(2), 168–70.

Epstein, J. L. (1995). School/family/community partnerships: Caring for the children we share. *Phi Delta Kappan, 76*(5), 701–12.

Epstein, J. L. (2001). *School, family, and community partnerships: Preparing educators and improving schools* (2nd ed.). Philadelphia: Westview Press.

Epstein, J., & Sanders, M. (2007). *Building school-community partnerships: Collaboration for student success*. Thousand Oaks, CA: Corwin.

Epstein, J. L., & VanVoorhis, F. L. (2001). More than minutes: Teachers' roles in designing homework. *Educational Psychologist, 36*(3), 181–93.

Escamilla, K., & Nathenson-Mejía, S. (2003). Preparing culturally responsive teachers: Using Latino children's literature in teacher education. *Equity & Excellence in Education, 36*(3), 238–48.

Ferreiro, E., & Teberosky, A. (1982). *Literacy before schooling*. Portsmouth, NH: Heinemann.

Finders, M., & Lewis, C. (1994). Why some parents don't come to school. *Educational Leadership 51*(8), 50–54.

Finter, B. (2015). *13 bridges children should know*. Munich: Prestel.

Fleer, M., & Williams-Kennedy, D. (2002). *Building bridges: Literacy development in young Indigenous children*. Australian Early Childhood Association.

Fleischer, C. (2000). *Teachers organizing for change: Making literacy-learning everybody's business*. Urbana, IL: National Council of Teachers of English.

Fleming, J., Catapano, S., Thompson, C. M., & Carrillo, S. R. (2016). *More mirrors in the classroom: Using urban children's literature to increase literacy*. Lanham, MD: Rowman & Littlefield.

Flippo, R. F. (2003). *Assessing readers: Qualitative diagnosis and instruction*. Portsmouth, NH: Heinemann.

Fountas, I., & Pinnell, G. S. (2008). *Leveled literacy intervention*. Portsmouth, NH: Heinemann.

Fox, M. (2008). *Reading magic: Why reading aloud to our children will change their lives forever* (2nd ed.). Wilmington, MA: Mariner Books.

Fox, M. (1997). *Whoever you are*. New York: Harcourt.

Freire, P. (1987). *Reading the world and the word*. New York: Praeger.

Friday, M. J. (2014, July 11). Why storytelling in the classroom matters. Edutopia blog.

Fruin, C. (2016, October 11). 6 ways technology can reinvent parent-teacher conferences. *EdSurge*. Retrieved from https://www.edsurge.com/news/2016-10-11-six-ways-technology-can-reinvent-parent-teacher-conferences

Fullan, M. (2001). *The new meaning of educational change*. New York: Teachers College Press.

Gaitan, C. D. (2004). *Involving Latino families in schools: Raising student achievement through home-school partnerships*. Thousand Oaks, CA: Corwin Press.

Gay, G. (2000). *Culturally responsive teaching: Theory, research, and practice*. New York: Teachers College Press.

Genishi, C., & Dyson, A. H. (2009). Children, language and literacy. New York: Teachers College Press.

Goldberg, C. (2001). Making schools work for low-income families in the 21st century. In S. Neuman & D. Dickinson (Eds.), *Handbook of early literacy research* (pp. 211–31). New York: Guilford Press.

Goldenberg, C., Reese, L., & Gallimore, R. (1992). Effects of literacy materials from school on Latino children's home experiences and early reading achievement. *American Journal of Education, 100*(4), 497–536.

Goodman, K. (2014). *What's whole in whole language in the 21st century?* New York: Garn Press.

Goodman, K., Shannon, P., Freeman, Y., & Murphy, S. (1988). *Report card on basal readers*. Katonah, NY: Richard C. Owens Publishers.

Goodman, Y. M., Watson, D., & Burke, C. (1996). *Reading strategies: Focus on comprehension* (2nd ed.). Katonah, NY: Richard C. Owen.

Grafwallner, P. (2017, March 8). Getting to know students through their histories. [Blog post]. Retrieved from https://www.edutopia.org/discussion/getting-know-students-through-their-histories.

Grogan, K. E., Henrich, C. C., & Malikina, M. V. (2014). Student engagement in after-school programs, academic skills, and social competence among elementary school students. *Child Development Research, 2014*(Article ID 498506), 1–9.

Guskey, T. R. (2002). *How's My Kid Doing? A Parent's Guide to Grades, Marks, and Report Cards. The Jossey-Bass Education Series*. Jossey-Bass, Inc., 989 Market Street, San Francisco, CA 94103-1741.

Harste, J. C. (2014). The art of learning to be critically literate. *Language Arts, 92*(2), 90–102.

Harste, J. C. (1986). *Composition and composition instruction as projected code: Understanding semiotic universals and practical theory*. Paper presented at New Directions in Composition Scholarship Conference, University of New Hampshire, Durham, NH.

Hart, B., & Risley, T. R. (1995). *Meaningful differences in the everyday experience of young American children.* Towson, MD: Paul H. Brookes.

Hearne, B., with Stevenson, D. (2000). *Choosing books for children: A commonsense guide.* Urbana: University of Illinois Press.

Heath, S. B. (1983). *Ways with words: Language, life and work in communities and classrooms.* Cambridge: Cambridge University Press.

Heath, S. B. (2010). Family literacy or community learning? Some critical questions on perspective. In K. Dunsmore & D. Fischer (Eds.), *Bringing literacy home* (pp. 15–41). Newark, DE: International Reading Association.

Henderson, A., & Mapp, K. (2002). A New wave of evidence: The impact of school. *Family, and Community Connections on Student Achievement.*

Henderson, A. T., Mapp, K. L., Johnson, V. R., & Davies, D. (2007). *Beyond the bake sale: The essential guide to family-school partnerships*. New York: New Press.

Henkes, K. (2008). *Chrysanthemum*. New York: HarperCollins.

Herold, J. (2011). Beginning and struggling readers: Engaging parents in the learning process. *Literacy Learning: The Middle Years, 19*(3), 40–51.

Hicks, D. (1998). Narrative discourses as inner and outer word. *Language Arts, 75*(1), 28–34.

Hoban, T. (1987). *I read signs*. New York: Greenwillow Books.

Hollingworth, S., Allen, K., Kuyok, K. A., Mansaray, A., Rose, A., & Page, A. (2009, September). An exploration of parents' engagement with their children's learning involving technologies and the impact of this in their family learning experiences. Becta. Retrieved from http://dera.ioe.ac.uk/10475/1/parents_engagement_children_final.pdf

Holmes, W. (2011). Using game-based learning to support struggling readers at home. *Learning, Media and Technology, 36*(1), 5–19.

Hong, S. (2011). *A Cord of Three Strands: A New Approach to Parent Engagement in Schools*. Harvard Education Press. 8 Story Street First Floor, Cambridge, MA 02138.

Hornsby, D. (2000). *A closer look at guided reading*. Armadale, AU: Eleanor Curtain.

Hornsby, D., & Wilson, L. (2010). *Teaching phonics in context*. Urbana, IL: NCTE.

Howard, K. M., & Lipinoga, S. (2010). Closing down openings: Pretextuality and misunderstanding in parent–teacher conferences with Mexican immigrant families. *Language & Communication, 30*(1), 33–47.

Hull, B., & Schultz, K. (Eds.). (2002). *School's out: Bridging out-of-school literacies with classroom practice*. New York: Teachers College Press.

International Literacy Association. (2002). *Family-school partnerships: Essential elements of literacy instruction in the United States*. Newark, NJ. Retrieved from https://www.literacyworldwide.org/docs/default-source/where-we-stand/family-school-partnerships-position-statement.pdf?sfvrsn=904ea18e_6

Isbell, R., Sobol, J., Lindauer, L., & Lowrance, A. (2004). The effects of storytelling and story reading on the oral language complexity and story comprehension of young children. *Early childhood education journal, 32*(3), 157–163.

Isenberg, J. P., & Jalongo, M. R. (1997). *Creative expression and play in early childhood*. Englewood Cliffs, NJ: Prentice Hall.

Janks, H. (2014). *Doing critical literacy: Texts and activities for students and teachers*. New York: Routledge.

Jason, L. A., Kuranasaki, K. S., Neuson, L., & Garcia, C. (1993). Training parents in a preventive intervention for transfer children. *Journal of Primary Prevention, 13*(3), 213–27.

Jensen, D. A. (2011). Examining teachers' comfort level of parental involvement. *Journal of Research in Education, 21*(1), 65–80.

Jensen, D. A., & Tuten, J. A. (2012). *Successful reading assessments and interventions for struggling readers: Lessons from literacy space*. New York: Palgrave Macmillan.

Jeynes, W. H. (2010). The salience of the subtle aspects of parental involvement and encouraging that involvement: Implications for school-based programs. *Teachers College Record*.

Johnson, A. S. (2010). The Jones family's culture of literacy. *Reading Teacher, 64*(1), 33–44.

Johnson, P., & Keier, K. (2010). *Catching readers before they fall: Supporting readers who struggle, K–4*. Portland, ME: Stenhouse.

Johnson-Parsons, M. (2010). Dreaming of collaboration. *Language Arts, 57*(1), 90–92.

Jonas, A. (1992). *The 13th clue*. New York: Greenwillow Books.

Keller, T., & Franzak, J. K. (2016). When names and schools collide: Critically analyzing depictions of culturally and linguistically diverse children negotiating their names in picture books. *Children's Literature in Education, 47*(2), 177–90.

Kelly, K. (n.d.). *19 questions to ask about afterschool programs*. Retrieved from https://www.understood.org/en/school-learning/tutors/afterschool-programs/checklist-questions-to-ask-when-looking-at-afterschool-programs

Keys, A. (2014). Family engagement in rural and urban Head Start families: An exploratory study. *Early Childhood Education Journal, 43*(1), 69–76.

King, J. E. (1994). The purpose of schooling for African American Children: Including cultural knowledge. In E. R. Hollins, J. E. King & W. C. Hayman, (Eds.), *Teaching diverse populations: Formulating a knowledge base* (pp. 25–56). Albany, NY: SUNY Press.

Kohn, A. (2006). Abusing research: The study of homework and other examples. *Phi Delta Kappa, 88*(1), 9–22.

Kreider, H., Caspe, M., & Hiatt-Michael, D. B. (2013). *Promising practices for engaging families in literacy.* Charlotte, NC: Information Age.

Kremer, K., Maynard, B., Polanin, J., Vaughn, M., & Sarteschi, C. (2015). Effects of after-school programs with at-risk youth on attendance and externalizing behaviors: A systematic review and meta-analysis. *Journal of Youth and Adolescence, 44*(3), 616–36.

Kress, G. (2005). *Before writing: Rethinking the paths to literacy.* New York: Routledge.

Kroeger, J., & Lash, M. (2011). Asking, listening, and learning: Toward a more thorough method of inquiry in home–school relations. *Teaching and Teacher Education, 27*(2), 268–77.

Kuepers, W. (n.d.). Crossing the divide: Bridges and bridging as integrative metaphors in organization and management studies. Retrieved from http://www.academia.edu/2167788/Crossing_the_Divide_-_Inter-Bridging_Bridges_and_bridging_as_metaphors_for_syntegrality_in_organization_studies

Ladson-Billings, G. J. (1999). Preparing teachers for diverse student populations: A critical race theory perspective. *Review of Research in Education, 24*, 211–47.

Lam, S. F., Chow-Yeung, K., Wong, B. P., Lau, K. K., & Tse, S. I. (2013). Involving parents in paired reading with preschoolers: Results from a randomized controlled trial. *Contemporary Educational Psychology, 38*(2), 126–135.

Lareau, A. (2000). *Home advantage: Social class and parental intervention in elementary education.* Lanham, MD: Rowman & Littlefield.

LaRocque, M. (2013). Addressing cultural and linguistic dissonance between parents and schools. *Preventing School Failure, 57*(2), 111–17.

Larrotta, C., & Gainer, J. (2008). Text matters: Mexican immigrant parents reading their world. *Multicultural Education, 16*(2), 45–48.

Latham, D. (2012). *Bridges and tunnels: Investigate feats of engineering.* White River Junction, VT: Nomad Press.

Lawrence-Lightfoot, S. (2003). *The essential conversation: What parents and teachers can learn from each other.* New York: Ballantine.

Lazar, A., Broderick, P., Mastilli, T., & Slostad, F. (1999). Educating teachers for parental involvement. *Contemporary Education, 70*(3), 5–10.

Lewison, M., Leland, C., & Harste, J. (2000). `Not in my classroom!' The case for using multi-view social issues books with children. *Australian Journal of Language and Literacy, 23*(1), 8.

Lin, G. (2012, April 6). Rethinking Tikki Tkki Tembo. *GraceLinBlog*. Retrieved from http://www.gracelinblog.com/2012/04/rethinking-tikki-tikki-tembo.html

Lipson, M. Y., & Wixson, K. K. (2003). *Assessment and instruction of reading and writing difficulty: An interactive approach* (3rd ed.). Boston: Allyn and Bacon.

Loera, G., Rueda, R., & Nakamoto, J. (2011). The association between parental involvement in reading and school and children's reading engagement in Latino families. *Literacy Research and Instruction, 50*(2), 133–55.

Lomax, R. (1996). On becoming assessment literate: An initial look at preservice teachers' beliefs and practices. Teacher *Educator, 31*(2), 292–303.

Lopez, M., & Caspe, M. (2014). *Family engagement in anywhere, anytime learning*. Harvard Family Literacy Project. Retrieved from http://media1.razorplanet.com/share/510991-7245/resources/834379_FamilyEngagementinAnywhereAnytimeLearning_HarvardFamilyResProj.pdf

Lopez, M., Caspe, M., & McWilliams, L. (2016). *Public libraries: A vital space for family engagement.* Cambridge, MA: Harvard Family Research Project.

López, L., Cohen, J., McAlister, K. T., Rolstand, K., & MacSwan, J. (2005). A look into the homes of Spanish-speaking preschool children. In *Proceedings of the 4th International Symposium on Bilingualism* (pp. 1378–1383). Somerville, MA: Cascadilla Press.

Luet, K. G. (2015). Disengaging parents in urban schooling. *Educational Policy 30*(5), 1–29.

Luke, A. (2011). Generalizing across borders: Policy and the limits of educational science. *Educational Researcher, 40*(8), 367–77.

Lyons, N. (1990). Dilemmas of knowing: Ethical and epistemological dimensions of teachers' work and development. *Harvard Educational Review, 60*(1), 159–190.

Mahoney, J. L. Lord, H., & Carryl, E. (2005). An ecological analysis of after school program participation and the development of academic performance and motivational attributes for disadvantaged children. *Child Development, 76*(4), 811–25.

Martin, E. J., & Hagan-Burke, S. (2002). Establishing home-school connections: Strengthening the partnership between families and school. *Preventing School Failure, 46*(2), 62–65.

Matson, S. F. (2013). Walking together into a third space: Using family literacy projects to learn more about students' paths. *English in Texas, 43*(1), 14–17.

McCarthey, S. J. (2000). Home-school connections: A review of the literature. *Journal of Educational Research, 93*(3), 145–53.

McCarthy, J. (2015, October 5). Parent-teacher conferences . . . or collaborative conversations? [Blog post]. Retrieved from https://www.edutopia. org/blog/parent-teacher-conferences-collaborative-conversations-john-mccarthy.

McGrath, K. (2014). Developing effective family-school partnerships: What can we learn from parents of children who struggle with reading? *College Reading Association Yearbook, 35*, 173–88.

McKenna, M. C., & Stahl, K. A. D. (2015). *Assessment for reading instruction.* New York: Guilford.

McKeough, A., Bird, S., Tourigny, E., Romaine, A., Graham, S., Ottmann, J., & Jeary, J. (2008). Storytelling as a foundation to literacy development for Aboriginal children: Culturally and developmentally appropriate practices. *Canadian Psychology/ Psychologie Canadienne, 49*(2), 148.

McTavish, M. (2007). Constructing the big picture: A working class family supports their daughter's pathways to literacy. *The Reading Teacher, 60*(5), 476–485.

Mehan, H. (1996). The construction of an LD student: A case study in the politics of representation. In M Silverstein & G. Urban (Eds.), *Natural histories of discourse* (pp. 253–276). Chicago: University of Chicago Press.

Mello, R. (2001). The power of storytelling: How oral narrative influences children's relationships in classrooms. *International Journal of Education & the Arts, 2*(1).

Miller, D. (2009). *The book whisperer: Awakening the inner reader in every child.* San Francisco: John Wiley and Sons.

Miller, G. E., & Nguyen, V. (2014). Family school partnering to support new immigrant and refugee families with children with disabilities. In L. Lo & D. B. Hiatt-Michael (Eds.), *Promising practices to empower culturally and linguistically diverse families of children with disabilities* (pp. 67–84). Charlotte, NC: Information Age.

Miller, S., & Pennycuff, L. (2008). The power of story: Using storytelling to improve literacy learning. *Journal of Cross-Disciplinary Perspectives in Education, 1*(1), 36-43.

Moll, L., Amanti, C., Neff, D., & Gonzalez, N. (2005). Funds of knowledge for teaching: Using a qualitative approach to connect homes and classrooms. In N. Gonzalez, L. C. Moll, & C. Amanti (Eds.), *Funds of knowledge: Theorizing practices in households, communities and classrooms* (pp. 71–88). Mahwah: NJ: Lawrence Erlbaum Associates.

Monk, I. (1998). *Hope.* Minneapolis: Lerner.

Morgan, H. (2015). Creating a class blog: A strategy that can promote collaboration, motivation, and improvement in literacy. *Reading Improvement, 52*(1), 27–31.

Mraz, K., & Hertz, C. (2015). *A mindset for learning: Teaching the traits of joyful, independent growth.* Portsmouth, NH: Heinemann.

Mueller, T. G. (2014). Learning to navigate the special education maze: A 3-tiered model for CLD family empowerment. In L. Lo & D. B. Hiatt-Michael (Eds.), *Promising practices to empower culturally and linguistically diverse families of children with disabilities* (pp. 3–14). Charlotte, NC: Information Age.

Mui, S., & Anderson, J. (2008). At home with the Johars: Another look at family literacy. *Reading Teacher, 62*(3), 234–43.

Munk, D. D., & Bursuck, W. D. (2001). What report card grades should and do communicate: Perceptions of parents of secondary students with and without disabilities. *Remedial and Special Education, 22*(5), 280–87.

Murillo, L. A. (2012). Learning from bilingual family literacies. *Language Arts, 90*(1), 18–29.

NCTE/ILA. (2009). *Standards for the assessment of reading and writing, revised edition.* Retrieved from http://www.ncte.org/standards/assessmentstandards

Oglan, G. R., & Elcombe, A. (2001). *Parent to parent: Our children, their literacy.* Urbana, IL: National Council of Teachers of English.

Ohio Department of Education. (2016). Kindergarten readiness assessment—literacy. Retrieved from http://education.ohio.gov/Topics/Early-Learning/Kindergarten/Ohios-Kindergarten-Readiness-Assessment

Ordonez-Jasis, R., & Flores, S. Y. (2011). Descubriendo historias/Uncovering stories: The literary worlds of latino children and families. In C. Compton-Lilly & S. Greene (Eds.), *Bedtime stories and book reports: Connection parent involvement and family literacy* (pp. 124–37). New York: Teachers College Press.

Paratore, J. R., & Jordan, G. (2007). Starting out together: A home-school partnership for preschool and beyond. *Reading Teacher, 60*(7), 694–96.

Patall, E. A., Cooper, H., & Robinson, C. (2008). Parent involvement in homework: A research synthesis. *Review of Educational Research, 78*(4), 1039–1101.

Pierce, C. M. (1969). Is bigotry the basis of the medical problems of the ghetto? In J. C. Norman (Ed.), *Medicine in the ghetto* (pp. 301–12). New York: Meredith Press.

Poza, L., Brooks, M. D., & Valdés, G. (2014). Entre familia: Immigrant parents' strategies for involvement in children's schooling. *School Community Journal, 24*(1), 119.

Purcell-Gates, V. (2006). Written language and literacy development: The proof is in the practice. *Research in the Teaching of English, 41*, 165–68.

Purcell-Gates, V., & Duke, N. K. (2004). Texts in the teaching and learning of reading. In J. Hoffman & D. Schallert (Eds.), *The texts in elementary classrooms* (pp. 3–20). Mahwah, NJ: Erlbaum.

Puzio, K., Newcomer, S., Pratt, K., McNeely, K., Jacobs, M., & Hooker, S. (2017). Creative failures in culturally sustaining pedagogy. *Language Arts, 94*(4), 223–32.

Recorvits, H. (2014). *My name is Yoon*. New York: Square Fish.

Reese, E. (2013, December). What kids learn from hearing family stories. *Atlantic*.

Reese, E., Robertson, S.-J., Divers, S., & Schaughency, E. (2015). Does the brown banana have a beak? Preschool children's phonological awareness as a function of parents' talk about speech sounds. *First Language, 35*(1), 54–67.

Reese, E., Sparks, A., & Leyva, D. (2010). A review of parent interventions for preschool children's language and emergent literacy. *Journal of Early Childhood Literacy, 10*(1), 97–117.

Reese, E., Suggate, S., Long, J., & Schaughency, E. (2010). Children's oral narrative and reading skills in the first 3 years of reading instruction. *Reading and Writing, 23*(6), 627–44.

Rhodes, L., & Dudley-Marling, C. (1998). *Readers and writers with a difference: A holistic approach to struggling readers and writers*. Portsmouth, NH: Heinemann.

Richards, S. B., Frank, C. L., Sableski, M. K., & Arnold, J. M. (2016). *Collaboration among professionals, students, families, and communities: Effective teaming for student learning*. London: Routledge.

Ringgold, F. (1991). *Tar beach*. New York: Scholastic.

Rios-Aguilar, C., Kiyama, J. M., Gravitt, M., & Moll, L. C. (2011). Funds of knowledge for the poor and forms of capital for the rich? A capital approach to examining funds of knowledge. *Theory and Research in Education, 9*(2), 163–84.

Robertson, S. J. L., & Reese, E. (2017). The very hungry caterpillar turned into a butterfly: Children's and parents' enjoyment of different book genres. *Journal of Early Childhood Literacy, 17*(1), 3–25.

Rochkind, J., Ott, A., Immerwahr, J., Doble, J., & Johnson, J. (2008). Lessons learned: New teachers talk about their jobs, challenges and long-range plans. Teaching in Changing Times. *Public Agenda, 3*.

Rogers, R. (2002). Through the eyes of the institution: A critical discourse analysis of decision making in two special education meetings. *Anthropology and Education Quarterly, 33*(1), 213-237.

Rowe, D., & Fain, J. (2013). Family backpack project: Responding to dual-language texts through family journals. *Language Arts 90*(6), 402–16.

Rowley, D. (2017, October 23). *Choosing the right after-school program for your kids*. Retrieved from https://www.care.com/c/stories/12446/choosing-the-right-after-school-program-for-y/

Rowsell, J. (2006). *Family literacy experiences: Creating reading and writing experiences that support classroom learning*. Markham, ON: Pembroke.

Ryndyk, O., & Johannessen, Ø. L. (2015). *Review of research literature on parenting styles, child rearing practices among Poles: Historical and contemporary perspectives*. Centre for Intercultural Communication, Stavanger, Norway. Retrieved from http://www.sik.no/uploads/sik-report-2015-3-pdf.pdf

Sadler, B., & Staulters, M. (2008). Beyond tutoring: After-school literacy instruction. *Intervention in School and Clinic, 43*(4), 203–9.

Sheldon, J., Arbreton, A., Hopkins, L., & Grossman, J. B. (2010). Investing in success: Key strategies for building quality in after-school programs. *American Journal of Community Psychology, 45*(3–4), 394–404.

Shockley, B., Michalove, B., & Allen, J. (1995). *Engaging families: Connecting home and school literacy communities*. Portsmouth, NH: Heinemann.

Short, K. (2013, January 7). Common Core State Standards: Misconceptions about text exemplars. *WOW Currents*. Retrieved from http://wowlit.org/blog/2013/01/07/common-core-state-standards-misconceptions-about-text-exemplars/

Short, K. G., Day, D., & Schroeder, J. (Eds.). (2016). *Teaching globally: Reading the world through literature*. Portland, ME: Stenhouse.

Silinskas, G., Niemi, P., Lerkkanen, M., & Nurmi, J. (2013). Children's poor academic performance evokes parental homework assistance—but does it help? *International Journal of Behavioral Development, 37*(1), 44–56.

Singer, I. B. (1978). *Nobel lecture.* Retrieved from https://www.nobelprize.org/nobel_prizes/literature/laureates/1978/singer-lecture.html

Sipe, L. R. (2008). *Storytime: Young children's literary understanding in the classroom*. New York: Teachers College Press.

Skilton-Sylvester, E. (2002). Literate at home but not at school: A Cambodian girl's journey from playwright to struggling writer. In L. Hull & K. Schultz (Eds.), *School's out: Bridging out-of-school literacies with classroom practice*. New York: Teachers College Press.

Smith, D. (2015, September 30). *How to choose the best after-school program*. Horizon Education Centers. Retrieved from https://www.horizoneducationcenters.org/blog/how-to-choose-the-best-after-school-program

Sonnenschein, S., & Munsterman, K. (2002). The influence of home-based reading interactions on 5-year-olds' reading motivations and early literacy development. *Early Childhood Research Quarterly, 17*(3), 318–37.

Souto-Manning, M., & Swick, K. J. (2006). Teachers' beliefs about parent and family involvement: Rethinking our family involvement paradigm. *Early Childhood Education Journal, 34*(2), 187–93.

Spielman, J. (2001). The family photography project: "We will just read what the pictures tell us." *Reading Teacher, 54*(8), 762–70.

Spitz, E. H. (1999). *Inside picture books*. New Haven, CT: Yale University Press.

Stevens, B. A., & Tollafield, A. (2003). Creating comfortable and productive parent/ teacher conferences. *Phi Delta Kappan, 84*(7), 521–24.

Street, B. V. (1995). *Social literacies: Critical approaches to literacy development, ethnology and education*. London: Longman.

Street, B. V. (Ed.). (2001). *Literacy development: Ethnographic perspectives*. London: Routledge.

Sutton, R., & Parravano, M. V. (2010). *A family of readers: The book lover's guide to children's and young adult literature*. Somerville, MA: Candlewick Press.

Swan, G. M., Guskey, T. R., & Jung, L. A. (2014). Parents' and teachers' perceptions of standards-based and traditional report cards. *Educational Assessment, Evaluation and Accountability, 26*(3), 289–299.

Taylor, D. (1982). Translating children's everyday uses of print into classroom practice. *Language Arts, 59*(6), 546–49.

Taylor, D. (1991). *Learning Denied*. Portsmouth, NH: Heinemann.

Taylor, D., & Dorsey-Gaines, C. (1988). *Growing up literate: Learning from inner-city families*. Portsmouth, NH: Heinemann.

Tejero-Hughes, M., Valle-Riestra, D. M., & Arguelles, M. E. (2008). The voices of Latino families raising children with special needs. *Journal of Latinos and Education, 7*(3), 241–57.

Tobin, J. (2014). Management and leadership issues for school building leaders. *International Journal of Educational Leadership Preparation, 9*(1), 1–14.

Tredway, L. (2003). *Community mapping: A rationale*. Principal Leadership Institute, University of California, Berkeley.

Tschannen-Moran, M. (2014). The interconnectivity of trust in schools. In D. Van Maele, P. B. Forsyth, & M. Van Houtte (Eds.), *Trust and school life* (pp. 57–81). Dordrecht: Springer Netherlands.

Tuten, J. (2007). "There's two sides to every story": How parents negotiate report card discourse. *Language Arts, 84*(4), 314–24.

Tuten, J., & Jensen, D. A. (2009). Matching texts and instructional strategies to struggling readers: Learning from teachers in an after-school tutoring program. *Reading Professor, 31*(2), 14–19.

Tyner, B. (2009). *Small-group reading instruction: A differentiated teaching model for beginning and struggling readers*. Newark, DE: International Reading Association.

Vitale-Reilly, P. (2018). *Supporting struggling learners: 50 instructional moves for the classroom teacher*. Portsmouth, NH: Heinemann.

Voss, M. (1996). *Hidden literacies: Young children learning at home and at school*. Portsmouth, NH: Heinemann.

Walker, J. M., Dempsey-Hoover, K. V., Whetsel, D. R., & Green, C. L. (2004, November). *Parental involvement in homework: A review of current research and its implications for teachers, after school program staff, and parent leaders.* Harvard Family Research Project, Cambridge, MA.

Wasik, B. H., Dobbins, D. R., & Herrmann, S. (2002). Intergenerational family literacy: Concepts, research, and practice. In S. B. Neuman & D.K. Dickinson (Eds.), *Handbook of early literacy research* (pp. 444–58). New York: Guilford Press.

Weiss, H., Lopez, M. E., & Rosenberg, H. (2010). Celebrating ten years of FINE (Family Involvement Network of Educators). *FINE Newsletter, 2*(4), 1–3.

Wells, G. (1980). *The meaning makers: Children learning language and using language to learn.* Portsmouth, NH: Heinemann.

Wells, G. (1986). *The meaning makers: Children learning language and using language to learn.* Heinemann Educational Books Inc., 70 Court St., Portsmouth, NH 03801.

What Works Clearinghouse. (n.d.). Institute of Education Sciences, U.S. Department of Education. Retrieved form https://ies.ed.gov/ncee/wwc/FWW/Results?filters=,Literacy#

White, C. L. (2009). "What he wanted was real stories, but no one would listen": A child's literacy, a mother's understandings. *Language Arts, 86*(6), 431–39.

Whitmore, K. F. (2015). Becoming the story in the joyful world of "Jack and the Beanstalk." *Language Arts, 93*(1), 25–37.

Whitmore, K. F., & Norton-Meier, L. A. (2008). Pearl and Rhonda: Revaluing mothers' literate lives to image new relationships between homes and elementary schools. *Journal of Adolescent and Adult Literacy, 51*(8), 450–61.

Whitmore, K. F., & Wilson, C. (2016). Photographs that cracked open narrow kindergarten writing practices for children and their teacher. In R. Meyer & K. Whitmore (Eds.), *Reclaiming early childhood literacies: Narratives of hope, power and vision* (pp. 255–58). New York: Routledge.

Williams, K. L., & Mohammed, K. (2009). *My name is Sangoel.* Grand Rapids, MI: Wm. B. Eerdmans.

Winston, L. (1997). *Keepsakes: Using family stories in elementary classrooms.* Portsmouth, NH: Heinemann.

Worthy, J. (1996). A matter of interest: Literature that hooks reluctant readers and keeps them reading. *Reading Teacher, 50*(3), 204–12.

Zigo, D. (2001). From familiar worlds to possible worlds: Using narrative theory to support struggling readers' engagements with texts. *Journal of Adolescent & Adult Literacy, 45*(1), 62–70.

Zimmerman, A. (2017, March 31). Goodbye parent-teacher conferences, hello poetry workshops: How New York City is redefining parent engagement. Chalkbeat. Retrieved from https://www.chalkbeat.org/posts/ny/2017/03/31/goodbye-parent-teacher-conferences-hello-poetry-workshops-how-new-york-city-is-redefining-parent-engagement/

Index

About the Authors

Jennifer Tuten is associate professor of literacy education at Hunter College, City University of New York. She teaches courses in literacy assessment, children's literature, and family–community engagement. In addition, she directs READ East Harlem/Hunter College, a collaborative professional development project uniting university literacy faculty with K–2 teachers and school leaders to support literacy teaching and learning. Her scholarship is practitioner focused, closely aligned with the challenges and opportunities facing teachers as they strive to meet the needs of literacy learners in urban schools. Prior to coming to Hunter College, she taught elementary and middle school in New York City; Hoboken, New Jersey; and London, England.

Deborah Ann Jensen was an associate professor in the Graduate Literacy Program at Hunter College, City University of New York. There she began Literacy Space, a two-semester assessment and intervention program in which struggling readers from elementary schools work with graduate students. As a literacy expert, Deborah publishes and presents in the areas of parental involvement and using children's literature across the curriculum. Recently, she retired from Hunter and now is a literacy consultant for ExpandED Schools in various after-school programs.

Charlene Klassen Endrizzi teaches literacy, family–school partnership, and children's literature courses for graduate and undergraduate students at Westminster College in Pennsylvania. Her research inquiries and publications with classroom teachers and preservice teachers focus on building family–school literacy partnerships and exploring global children's literature. She writes blogs with colleagues for the University of Arizona's Worlds of Words (www.wowlit.org), an international children's literature website for teachers. Before teaching in Westminster's School of Education, she taught bilingual and immigrant fourth through sixth graders in high-needs schools in Fresno, California. She lives in New Wilmington, Pennsylvania, with her husband, George, and teenage son, Bryce.